Rebuilding Trust in a Marriage:

-2 books in 1-

A Complete Guide to Rebuilding Your Relationship, Overcome Codependency, Resolve Conflict and Improve Intimacy

CLARISSA HAMPTON-JONES

© **Copyright 2019 by Clarissa Hampton-Jones**
All rights reserved.

This document is geared towards providing exact and reliable information in regards to the topic and issue covered. The publication is sold with the idea that the publisher is not required to render accounting, officially permitted, or otherwise, qualified services. If advice is necessary, legal or professional, a practiced individual in the profession should be ordered.
- From a Declaration of Principles which was accepted and approved equally by a Committee of the American Bar Association and a Committee of Publishers and Associations.

In no way is it legal to reproduce, duplicate, or transmit any part of this document in either electronic means or printed format. Recording of this publication is strictly prohibited and any storage of this document is not allowed unless with written permission from the publisher. All rights reserved.
 The information provided herein is stated to be truthful and consistent, in that any liability, in terms of inattention or otherwise, by any usage or abuse of any policies, processes, or directions contained within is the solitary and utter responsibility of the recipient reader. Under no circumstances will any legal responsibility or blame be held against the publisher for any reparation, damages, or monetary loss due to the information herein, either directly or indirectly.
 Respective authors own all copyrights not held by the publisher.

The information herein is offered for informational purposes solely and is universal as so. The presentation of the information is without a contract or any type of guarantee assurance.

The trademarks that are used are without any consent, and the publication of the trademark is without permission or backing by the trademark owner. All trademarks and brands within this book are for clarifying purposes only and are owned by the owners themselves, not affiliated with this document.

Table of Contents

How to Help Your Spouse Heal From Your Affair

Chapter 1: Introduction 8
Chapter 2: Relationships and Infidelity 14
Chapter 3: Society today is fertile ground for traitors 25
Chapter 4: Betrayal has no gender and age 34
Chapter 5: Warning signs of a betrayal 44
Chapter 6: How to face a betrayal 58
Chapter 7: Consequences of a betrayal on children 70
Chapter 8: After the storm the calm 81
Chapter 9 "What to do to get happy again" .. 104
Chapter 10: Examples for setting up a shooting path 121
Chapter 11: I still believe in our relationship 132
Chapter 12: Ten Steps to Happiness 147
Chapter 13: Conclusions 167

CODEPENDENCY NO MORE

Chapter 1: Anatomy of Codependent Relationships 173

Chapter 2: You Are Not Insane—You Are Codependent... 182

Chapter 3: Comprehension of Jealousy-Driven, Controlling Behavior 197

Chapter 4: How Can Codependency Ruin Relationships? 206

The Development of a Codependent 207
Enter Codependency 212

Chapter 5: Warning Signs of Codependency 216

Chapter 1: Stages of Codependency 224

STAGE ONE: 227
STAGE TWO: 233
STAGE THREE: 236
STAGE FOUR: 240

Chapter 2: How to Overcome Codependency 243

Chapter 3: Are You Still Codependent? ... 259

What is it Like to Live with Codependency?... 264

Chapter 4: Heal All Your Relationships...268

How Do You Bring Boundaries into This Mix? 272

Chapter 5: Ten Step Program for a New Life without Codependency........................... 280

Recognize That You Are Using These Behaviors to Cope with the Harms Caused to You 280

Understand That Codependent Behaviors are Based in Shame 285

Be Aware of the Shadows of Shame and How They Undermine Your Ability to See Your Worth 294

Acknowledging and Embracing All Their Feelings of Betrayal and Hurt 297

Understand How Partners Engage in Codependent Relationships 300

Developing the Mind-Body-Spirit Connection 307

Join a Group That Focuses on Codependency Recovery 312

Increase Understanding of Addiction and Codependency 318

Seek Counseling from a Licensed and Qualified Therapist Who is Familiar with Codependency 327

Practice Mindfulness and Self-Compassion.... 329

Chapter 6: Conclusion..........................336

How to Help Your Spouse Heal From Your Affair

A Guide to Rebuilding Your Marriage

Chapter 1: Introduction

"My wife doesn't understand that my hurt is real and my wounds are deep."

"Just after acknowledging that he cheated, he said he had been forgiven by God. It must be put behind us and we should get back together."

There comes a moment when the unfaithful person comes clean about their affair and instantly feels relieved. They must have kept the affair in the dark for weeks, months or even years. They may feel free of their shame or guilt. They don't have to stay in hiding anymore.

The betrayed spouse, on the other hand, fears their worst nightmare has come true. Their world turns upside down. It is a very difficult, crushing place to be in, because they don't know how to navigate through this. The irrationality and unfairness of the situation can rip their heart out while the other partner is experiencing relief.

Let's begin with the unfaithful partner realizing that coming clean or being exposed doesn't end their duty of loyalty and honesty towards their spouse. This is far from the truth. Ideally, you need to be present for your partner, and everything you need to know is discussed in this book. The author invites both parties in the relationship to get on the healing train.

It's important to be aware of the sufferings caused to people after discovering betrayal in their relationship. It can drastically impact mental health. People who are in great suffering may reach a point where they experience a mental breakdown. They may become ill in the face of dealing with pain. When the pain is too difficult to deal with, people may attempt to distract themselves by staying busy, drinking or acting up in front of their loved ones, and try to suppress the condemnation, shame and the feeling of inadequacy.

Another likely possibility is turning bitter and resentful towards the unfaithful partner. This can result in the couple being stuck. The betrayed may get frustrated that they are not getting the complete information, and the unfaithful won't cooperate. There is some level of bitterness that each person will go through in this situation. Your lack of self-awareness can frustrate you. It is likely that both of you will not always behave in a way that is particularly healing. But there is a difference between ending up stuck versus passing through the hallway of bitterness. The decision will have to come from you to not stay there. Countless people choose to remain bitter, not being accountable for their own emotions. Especially when they are victims of someone else's terrible immorality. However, you just need to pass through this stage, and something better awaits you. After suffering this great pain, you will love deeper and better. You will love in spite of all the challenges or circumstances you have faced. Eventually, you will arrive at a great place of deep gratitude, connection, and contentment in your life.

    A person's conditioning and their family environment while growing up plays a very important role in their present life. Almost everyone comes from families where there are fights, secrecy, guilt or shame. There may have been no channel to communicate about anything such as your daily struggles, or boyfriends or girlfriends. So, your conditioning is such that you don't openly express how you feel, and you may get awkward when someone else expresses their feelings for you. Ask yourself if you were allowed to state your needs and expectations, or you were focused on what others wanted from you. Evaluate if you were raised to be loyal towards others, or you were raised to do what was right for you. Everyone generally advises you to do what you want and what makes you happy. This statement exists without the consequences of how it will affect those you love. You are a part of the large embedded community, and you can't always pursue what you want without discerning the needs of others. Did you learn to love from people who were protecting you, or did you have to flee away for protection? Were you allowed to cry out loud or laugh out loud in your family?

Were you touched, were you rocked, or were you beaten or invaded or violated? What were the relationship boundaries like in your family? What was your place in the family?

When you come out of your family after having grown up, what do you look for? Whether it is comfort, protection, and love, or the need for space and longing to escape or travel or wander around. These questions are deep-rooted in shaping your relationships. How you will react to being cheated or if you will ever cheat or not depends on the complexities of your past. All of us need security and adventures in our relationships. But one may need something more than the other. Attachment can be rooted in security, insecurity or anxiety. The ability to rely on someone who can share your distress, your joy and can respond to it appropriately without neglect, overemphasis on themselves; without pretending that it's for you when it is actually for them. A secure attachment is when we have a person who provides us with enough bandwidth to explore and is there for us, and your relationship won't fall apart no matter what. If this is missing from a person's life, they may develop insecure attachments. It can be constant checking on the other person, going after them, picking fights to grab their attention and so on. You may become the pursuer in the relationship who always wants more or who needs to be assured or affirmed of the other person's intentions. You can also be a withholder who always withholds the conflict or fears of being invaded. You may have learned to intentionally not come too close in order to save yourself from disappointment. Our attachments today are adaptive of the moments we were experiencing something bad earlier. This only becomes a problem when you start doing this with someone who genuinely cares about you, loves you dearly, and you are still responding to them from the place in your past where you learned it's better to stay distant to keep yourself safe. Usually, our strategies that we devised at the time to deal with a certain situation were useful then but may become redundant now.

Chapter 2: Relationships and Infidelity

A successful life is a melting pot of a lot of ingredients, such as a good career, loving and caring people, healthy relationships and a good standard of living. In our lives, we can prioritize one over the other but can never completely ignore a single one. Each of these things makes an individual's world whole. A healthy, fulfilling and faithful relationship can help you face a bad day at work with a smile. When people are in love, everything seems possible. Problems get shared between you and your partner so that they don't seem like a big deal. A good relationship is central to every person's life. Every species that exists on our planet wants to keep itself safe. The front part of our brain controls impulses and helps us think critically and ensure our safety. The Medulla helps to scan danger and be alert if situations demand so. There is another thing that human seeks to feel safe, which is human attachment. They attach themselves to feel secure and to share their emotions and thoughts. As babies, we need parents or caregivers to take care of us. As adults, we need someone to attach ourselves to. There are a few people who don't fathom any relationships and keep themselves detached. They don't like to commit, and instead stay alone. That is a personal choice. The majority of people believe there is that one perfect person for them who will be the key they are looking for and will unlock all the doors of happiness and celebration in each other's lives.

    Many find that perfect person in high school, or at work, or while riding a train or may still be searching. In today's technological world, people put their pride on the line in the name of online dating. Rejection can be so immediate and palpable, but you merely have to swipe right to find a date. To understand more about this new day and age love, there is no virtual risk. In case you swiped for a person and the other person doesn't swipe for you, they will never even know about you. Online dating provides a pool of choices and opportunities. Everyone is surrounded by potential mating alternatives and science says you are looking at them.

About 50 years ago, researchers looked into why people persist to stay in relationships to understand the ultimate driving force in a relationship. Now, this brings a lot of factors to light. A prevalent theory at the time was John Thibaut and Harold Kelley's theory of interdependence. According to them, dependence is based on two processes. First is satisfaction. This measures how much your partner is meeting your most important needs. The second process is the quality of alternatives available around you. This means how desirable is your next best alternative to this relationship. A similar theory that can help to understand relationships is an investment scale. This is probably the most widely used scale today. This theory uses investment or resources that tie up the relationship which would get lost if the relationship ended. The higher the investment, the greater the loss. The more people are involved in a relationship at a given period, the more damage control needs to be done once the relationship falls apart. An important observation here is that both theories evaluate the quality of an alternative available to an individual. Everyone puts value in finding the best match for them. We tend to devalue this evaluation when we are in a consciously satisfying and deeper relationship. But the minute the security begins to falter, we start to look for the next best alternative.

The whole dating and relationship scenario has seen a major shift. There is little to no stigma left around divorce. People accept failed relationships more than successful relationships. But the worst venom is infidelity. When infidelity strikes in a relationship, it introduces the affected to a whole new world of pain. It is the worst feeling in the world. Infidelity happens to be the most prevalent reason for breaking off relationships, and has increased multifold in recent times. Your spouse or your partner, who has been your rock, the person who you shared several years with, had an affair. It smashes your whole life apart. The people who surround you make it even worse. It's heartbreaking to see your life getting gossiped about.

The situation is no better than a nightmare. After the initial shock of the situation comes the anger. The anger is complemented with disgust and hatred. There is a breach of trust in your relationship. The situation affects not just the couple but those in their families.

Betrayal is betrayal. When two people come together in a relationship, they share emotions and feelings that they don't share with anyone else. If one decides to go outside the relationship and seek comfort and share their life with someone else, this is infidelity. This breach can be sexual or emotional. Sexual intimacy with someone other than your partner is painful. It hits you hard. It can happen with just sex or just a physical act. The offender may try to convince the betrayed by calling it a one-time mistake.

The other type of infidelity is emotional. For a long period, this wasn't even considered a form of betrayal. To be emotionally intimate with someone other than your partner can be easily denied. It can be perceived as a close friendship. It may or may not be sexual, but being sexually intimate here is not the key. The important fact is trusting someone else enough to share your feelings and your life with, not your partner. The connection here might be much stronger. The emotions involved are much more complex. Usually, the offender is just at the brink of breaking into a sexual relationship with this other person, but has not been involved in it yet. But the emotions and feelings are all there. The offender can easily argue that the relationship is a close friendship and confuse the betrayed by calling their feelings irrational. Whether there is an actual breach of trust or emotions is still not known to the betrayed. Where the betrayed suffers internally by not being able to express the doubt, along with the offender denying their mistake, the relationship falters and falls apart. It won't be wrong to say that this kind of intimacy is much harder to recover from than a sexual relationship.

Betrayal is very individualistic. It can differ from situation to situation. What can be perceived as infidelity by one may not be a betrayal for the other. The responses and reactions of the people around us impact everything that happens in our lives from that point on. It is statistically true that about 60% of people have suicidal thoughts after infidelity. With the relationship put in a maze, the betrayed loses the ability to trust their partner or anyone else. The feeling sucks you into a period of depression. The person is filled with self-doubt and loses confidence in terms of judging someone's character. There is a constant feeling of rage and hurt combined that takes a long time to heal or recover from. The feeling of being betrayed again depends on the person who is suffering from it. In a new relationship, if the partner cheats, it can be easier to let go. "There are plenty of fish in the sea." "She didn't deserve you." These are some common responses and it is definitely hurtful but can be learned from, and people can move on. If someone is in a longer-term relationship, the hurt it causes to the betrayed can vary leaps and bounds. This is when someone's nature will dictate how much they get plunged into darkness. Some people complain of not being able to remove the pictures mentally. Some suffer from sleepless nights. Some may get depressed. The kind of feelings that may hit the affected can't be easily understood. No amount of reading human psychology can prepare you to face these circumstances.

It is difficult to control the anxiety. The pressing need to check your partner's mobile phone, endless fights with the partner, feelings of self-doubt, trying to find an escape from the situation or trying to reason with the behavior of your offending partner. This can be termed as relationship trauma and is very similar to Post Traumatic Stress Disorder (PTSD). The parts of a day or people that you would have normally enjoyed, like going to the park, visiting your friends or family, become difficult to bear since it's hard to face anyone. Besides this feeling, the thoughts of "what's wrong with me" and "why did this happen to me" are even more heart-wrenching.

Alternatively, the actual focus should be on what went wrong. The relationship between these two people sometimes has nothing to do with cheating. The relationship can be perfectly fine, yet still someone goes outside to seek comfort. It is much easier to say that the offender cheated because they had a bad relationship. These days, with easy divorces, if people have poor relationships, they seek divorce. However, if they go outside marriage, it usually means they don't want to lose their original partner. There are some things they don't want to let go, but still go out of the marriage to seek something that is missing. This complexity is usually ignored since it is difficult to describe and explain. No theory of infidelity can explain the absolute nature of it in terms of how it affects the relationship. Infidelity often manages to strain a relationship, no matter how much a relationship may adapt to it.

We try to realize the reason why someone tries to break free from a relationship and risks to hurt someone who they have vowed to be with. The vows to stay together, have children, have a perfect house and intended job. What changes and triggers someone to break free from the shackles is the fault of no one but the offending partner. It's not you. You feel shattered and gutted because socially and personally it breaks everything down. It's amazing how one day we wish for certain things, and the next day we may want to be completely detached from them and perceive them as something imprisoning us. How a person who is completely sexually detached from their original partner is lustful and eager and can't bring it home. Matrimony started by being an imposition on women to mark exclusiveness. This has now changed to dual gender commitment. To put it simply, instead of giving more freedom to women, we have taken away freedom from men. Ideally, we need to embrace the complexity of relationships and what the infidelity of the relationship is feasting on, rather than being superficial and saying the easy thing to say and doing the easy thing to do. It is wrong to define infidelity in an ambit of extremity and describing that as the norm and ultimately measuring every circumstance in that light. There is a difference between trying to understand and trying to justify. It is necessary to understand the circumstance and then act rather than passing judgments, being narrow-minded and engaging in discrimination against the offending partner, because this won't help partners, families and their children.

Chapter 3: Society today is fertile ground for traitors

The world has completely changed today compared to even the past decade alone. Social media platforms and applications like Tinder, Bumble and so on have made communication very easy. With easy communication, there is a pathway to easy connections. These connections develop into relationships and since these relationships have lower tangibility, they may not last long. Although it is not a conclusive statement, this is what is generally noticed by experts. Again, the whole scenario of online dating is not to be blamed for this. It is a matter of personal choice.

For relationships that begin online, about 17% result in marriage. There have always been rules in a marriage or a relationship. What is perceived as friendship and what is crossing the line has to be mutually agreed on and clear. But these rules have experienced a major shift in the past decade. From the dialed-up internet age to the fastest network accessed by almost everyone, the dating game has also had an upgrade. There are over 360 million people who have accounts on Facebook, 69 million on Twitter, over one billion people on Instagram and so on in the year 2019. All it takes is to Google the name of a person you wish to connect with, and with a little information, you can access their pictures and a large portion of their lives. With this information, it is relatively easier to strike up a conversation, think and carefully craft the conversation, make an impression and build a relationship. If a person had met their partner online and isn't satisfied with their current relationship, they may think to look for another partner online. Even if you start a conversation with someone without any preconceived notion of cheating on your partner, it can develop into something more than friendship without you realizing it. In your head, you may have conceived the idea that it is possible to have a relationship with this person someday in the future. It is possible to fall in love with someone's words and get really intimate really fast. This serves our right and our need for belonging and intimacy.

In the past, the opportunities that were not available then are easily available now. A section of society exists that exercises gender dominance and finds it appropriate to cheat while staying married to their partners. It is a shame that people hide behind the covers of culture and religion and find it appropriate to get involved with more than one person. The problem here is not just one sex being allowed to have more partners, it's the forbidden dance of the contrary. This narcissism definitely stems from cultural dominance and precedents in the families that raise them. Infidelity is considered morally acceptable in various parts of the world.

The quality of our lives is defined by the success or failure we see in our relationships. No one on their death bed wishes for an extra day of work. Our lives revolve around the love we get from our parents growing up, our friends and ultimately our partners. If we talk about relationships in general, not much change has been noticed in the relationship of a baby with his caregivers, of siblings or with your doctor. The relationship that has seen an exorbitant change in recent times is the couple. Sexuality, which was earlier rooted in procreation, is now replaced with desire, lust and connection. A couple together provides each other with economic and social support, children, a good standard of living and so on. In addition to being one another's best friend, confidant, intellectual equal, passionate lover, inspiration and the list goes on. It takes lesser requirements to start a business than the amount of pressure couples today feel. Everyone seeks a lot more than what they used to, and this is before technology entered your bedrooms. A couple has had so many experiences, it's so complex to analyze a couple and disintegrate every problem because of the complexity of the circumstances involved.

There is no school for a relationship. A lot of people feel doubtful at various stages in a relationship with no one to guide them, and all this happens because there is no one who they can turn to for advice. Imagine the pressure when people find love in their twenties and wish for it to stay for the next fifty years with unconditional love and passion and commitment. While the format of a swiping culture is great, it brings a lot of choices to people, but it also brings the anxiety of how to know this person is the one when there are hundreds of other matches that you haven't contacted yet. There is a major lack of face-to-face communication to build serious relationships. With the introduction of television, mobile phones, laptops, and more and more devices, our time is taken by technology rather than building personal connections. Major concerns of people's lives are rather discussed over texts and then people complain about misunderstandings. When people wish for a relationship which has everything they dream of, they should also inculcate the resilience it takes to make it work.

The ups and downs, the fights and vacations and betrayals; it is imperative to grow through the struggles for a couple to withstand the challenges a relationship brings. And this spirit is exactly what is missing.

The majority of people struggle in naming one perfect, ideal relationship they look up to. You can immediately name your favorite businessman, favorite athlete or favorite musician. If you want to make a business successful, you need to fall in love with your customer, perceive everything from their eyes, and deliver quality every single time. Similarly, for anyone who wants to have an intimate relationship, there are no perfect models to learn from. So, let's start by discussing what goes wrong in a relationship. When there is a paradigm shift from what you are giving to what you are getting in the relationship, the problems start to arise. In couple's therapy, no one comes to look deeper into their lives; they come to fix their partners. People don't want to change themselves. The notion that 'you are responsible for my happiness and because of you, I am miserable' is what needs a turnaround. This notion makes you angry and resentful, and with the increasing emotions, you as a couple are drifting apart. The distance then may bring someone else in the picture, who will understand you better than your partner does, leading to infidelity. There is a plethora of options to choose from. It is so simple to put a password on the phone and change it now and then, meet new people online and form connections or delete a conversation on the phone. This makes cheating easy, and so some people jump in to get a piece of the action. People who cheat may have ruined some lives, but can move ahead to make other relationships faster today, and this is where the biggest setback of online dating lies. People constantly lie on the internet. A lot of people lie about their ages, preferences, height, weight or any other personal details, and it's so easy to fall into the trap.

People who have their accounts on social media are already a part of online love. If a man leaves his sleeping wife and goes to have sex with another woman, it is cheating. Some may agree if he sits on his couch and talks to the other woman about his thoughts and emotions, it is also cheating. If a man appreciates a woman's social media account and spends a lot of time checking her out, is that also cheating? There are a lot of questions that need to be navigated in a relationship today. There is no set questionnaire that you can fill out to know everything you need to know about your partner.

Everything cannot be easily articulated. Some things are felt and not said. But these factors impact every relationship today. Imagine how well relationships can work if one is open about every infatuation, every feeling and every emotion that erupts in their mind, and the partner understands them and stays by their side. Fantasizing while having sex, oral sex, attempting to seduce, sending flirty messages constitute cheating. Society today plays a major role in people's minds. People may have a cheating gene in them since forever, but may have not been able to tap into it and act upon it due to lack of opportunity. If you put them in today's dating scene, they may find it easy to cheat on people. Ultimately the paradox of blame lies on both society and the traitor. It is not fair to hold one responsible singularly.

Chapter 4: Betrayal has no gender and age

All people are different. When moving from adolescence to adulthood, society imbibes various postulations into the mind of an individual. There are so many cultural influences, religious beliefs and individualistic behavior that shapes a person's life. Society, in general, is plagued by failed marriages, divorces, unhealthy and abusive relationships. Every age brings its new challenges. In the teen years, a person attempts to get aligned with their sexuality while struggling with inner insecurities and external influences. This is a sensitive age and relationships at this age can afford to be more experimental. Precarious bonds or bad experiences can impact and shape future relationships. Immaturity and jealousy are inevitable. It is a phase of exploring newer things and trying to break free. Being young and being free is a wondrous feeling and fills your heart with excitement. When parents try to monitor the behavior, it is perceived as bondage. Accepting their parents' advice and acting on it seems to be the last thing teenagers want to do. The tendency to break free develops and the same gets reflected on the relationship. The urge to be free, careless, independent and wild clouds the mind, and young people may seek the same in other relationships later on. Sticking with one single, person while imagining there are a lot of options in the world, seems less exciting. They search for freedom in friendships and relationships, which may dwindle if they are tied down. However, having multiple relationships also clears up what a person wants in their lives, without hurting anyone's feelings if kept a secret.

    A young adult who is just coiled in a relationship and wishes to build a family unit faces various emotions. To build a relationship, various hurdles need to be passed. Acceptance of the partner, managing finances and getting along with each other's families, to name a few. The innate needs to break free from these shackles of responsibilities, and enduring commitment can push a person or bring him to the edge of looking for an escape.

Every human being has a flair for freedom. Some can fight it, and some cannot. Therefore, cheating is a matter of personal choice devoid of age or gender. While struggling with managing a new life, if there is someone who promises comfort and an out from the routine, then one may be drawn to that. Those who refrain from settling down are in fear of growing up. These people refuse to commit and get into long term relationships, and may be likely to jump from one relationship to another just because they don't want to be tied down.

Around the middle years, an adult who is in a relationship, which has been sustained for several years, comes to follow a routine. Routine by definition is a series of actions that are being followed repeatedly. Everyone despises getting into a rut and many fall into it without realizing. It is one of the most feared scenarios in a relationship. The matter of losing something despite having everything is inexplicable, and the person starts questioning the relationship to the point that he yearns to look outside of the relationship. The charm and passion that seems to have lost its luster in this old relationship, which they then seek through this other person. The betrayal at this stage is hurtful because of so many invested years. The man turns to younger women to experience the newness that they lack. It's equivalent to reliving their youth. On the other hand, the woman who is almost entering the menopausal phase of her life and questioning her womanhood and feeling undesired, chases after someone else to get in touch with her sexuality and to feel desired again. She craves attention more than ever, and if the opportunity arises, she might go for it.

It is believed that men cheat more than women. But women have come to be equals in this race and tend to cheat just as much as men. Men cheat due to falling into a routine. They may feel unsatisfied or under-appreciated. They may find an opportunity to cheat with few chances of getting caught. For example, thinking it is only a one-time thing. They may get addicted to pornography. There is no breathing space in the relationship. Women may cheat due to insecurities such as approaching an older age or changing bodies. Women are usually more accommodating and are more suppressed by family and social pressures than men. She may get too saturated with the impositions and look to break free. She may feel she doesn't get the attention or care she deserves from her partner. The other person is not sensitive to her sexual needs. In some cases, she may just be bored. For men, it's more of an egotistic matter of getting the woman to like them. For women, it may be a perfect way to get their emotional pangs satisfied.

Statistically, around 53% of people who cheat on their spouses are married. Only 6% of cheaters confess to cheating on their spouses. Men tend to leave women more often than the reverse by 22%, when they find out about their cheating. About 35% of women live in denial of their men cheating and refuse to act on it. Women can cheat better than men because they are better liars. 8% to 15% of children haven't been fathered by the person who is considered the biological father. Both men and women are likely to cheat.

In cases of cheating, there is a huge communication gap between the couple. Communication is key in any relationship. Differences arise when one doesn't speak their heart out and reserves inhibitions in their minds to protect the other's feelings. This leads to accumulating emotions that burst out and cause serious fights. The accumulation of problems is worse than solving individual and isolated battles. By working out each battle, the gap doesn't widen, and understanding and compatibility grow with time. However, reserving doubts in the mind and bearing questionable or unsatisfactory behavior from your partner just pushes you to get exhausted from the relationship.

Maybe your partner is unable to provide for your financial needs. Most people are unapologetically materialistic, and they must have their requirements fulfilled. They yearn for maintaining a standard of living and derive pleasure in spending money. Women are accused of being gold diggers; however, men can be just the same. There are as many dependent men as there are women. Educational loans, childcare loans and business loans impact the stress levels of a person, and a pressuring spouse is the last thing they can handle. Before entering in the relationship, financial matters must be necessarily discussed and either one should be able to provide for the other's needs, or they must be equals with no burden on a single person to fulfill every whim of the other person.

Constant fights and misunderstandings can pressure anyone to leave their present state and look for better avenues. With the number of opportunities available for people, no one likes to stay unhappy. Everyone itches to move forward in life, and if the people in the relationship refuse to reflect on the reason of the misunderstanding and let the gap grow, the other person outside the relationship who simply agrees with them more will tempt them to fall out of love. Fights help people to make their relationship stronger. However, when the fights are recurring and they aren't resolved properly, you can anticipate that one might set their heart on someone else who isn't so complicated to deal with.

Abuse, whether it is emotional or physical, makes a person fall out of love. Abusive relationships bring the victim a world of pain. Emotional abuse happens when one person manipulates, controls and isolates their partner and makes them helpless. Their growth is almost stinted, and their anxiety and stress levels are high, while being around the other person or not. Physical abuse is literal in the sense of hurting the person by slapping, beating or other forms of violence. A person can turn abusive due to plenty of reasons, such as having a bad reputation at work, low self-esteem, and general hatred and so on. The other person must prepare an exit plan immediately in such situations. Physical abuse puts a person off almost immediately. Such a relationship preludes its end, but a relationship infected by emotional abuse may take some time to get out of. The person may find solace in someone else who appears to be their well-wisher or an old friend who is familiar and consoling. The longer the period of misbehavior, the higher the chances of cheating.

Betrayal hits hard and leaves a wreck behind, which makes it extremely difficult to get past. It leaves the victim shook and their soul stained. The one who is cheated on gets filled with self-doubt. The fear of what they failed to provide to the person who cheated is ever-daunting. This is followed by an extreme amount of anger, which surfaces due to the unfairness of the situation. The fear of the unknown and unstable future, at that moment, clouds the brain. One needs to think about rebuilding one's life again. In some situations, it can be harder than anything else. In longer relationships, codependency happens to be natural and it is very hard to get over. The conflicting feelings of not being able to live with this person and the hatred to see their face confuses, irritates and disturbs you.

At different ages, betrayal is dealt with differently. In the adolescent years, the victim behaves the most violently and recklessly in the situation. Due to a lack of maturity, the affected may turn suicidal or clinically depressed. The manner to deal with the situation doesn't come naturally to them, so like every other emotion, reaction to this situation is heightened and they may act up. As a young adult faced by betrayal, it fills the person with suspicion about themselves. The foundation of every new relationship is affected by this failed one. If a person is cheated on in their middle age, they try to dust it under the carpet after sustaining the initial shock. They both try to come to an agreement to stay together or end up in a divorce in a mature manner. Usually, the couple has children and they are the priority for every parent. The focus shifts towards them and their well-being is always a concern.

Chapter 5: Warning signs of a betrayal

Trust your intuitions. The majority of cases of infidelity hide in the dark because the offender is never caught. Perhaps, the person is very careful or the one who is cheated on is blinded by the love of the unfaithful and fails to see the deed. However, there will be some oddities in the behavior of the unfaithful and you need to see them. These behavioral changes should not go unnoticed, and attention and alertness are imperative. Ignoring the signs and staying in denial will end up in hurting the soul more than facing it. The lies and wrong deeds just accumulate to the point that they become hard to ignore and there is little to no hope left for the relationship to survive. You must look for these silent signs without tipping them off. There are plenty of ways to know if your partner is cheating on you or not, but you must not lose context. Some odd behaviors don't mean your spouse is sleeping with someone else or is connected to someone else emotionally. You must look at the bigger picture and look for changes in the patterns of behavior. Be patient to understand the reason for something out of the norm.

Your partner is suddenly very possessive of their mobile phone, laptop or any electronic device and refuses to let you touch them. You should be concerned when they are being more secretive about this than before. It clearly points towards their aversion to you finding out about who they are communicating with. In times of technological indulgence when it is not hard to maintain proximity with anyone, mobile phones play a significant role in increasing a connection or maintaining one. They have changed their computer passwords and shut down their computer when you are around them while they are working. Be aware if you notice late-night phone calls and them becoming secretive about the caller. It shouldn't feel normal to keep a check on your spouse's phone obsessively for signs of a potential third party. If the person has somehow become compulsive about the whereabouts of their phone or is getting calls that they refuse to take in front of you, this can be a matter of concern.

Your spouse is changing their dressing style or is concerned about their looks more than usual. Perhaps they are spending extra time in the gym to get in shape, or taking extra time to get ready in the morning, or dressing impressively for what appears to be casual outings. This is in no way definitive of a person who is looking for someone to chat with, but if these occurrences take place in your mundane routines, this may be a sign. If you find yourself in this situation, it's advisable to be alert and watch your partner's activities closely and attempt to have open conversations about your concerns.

They are losing interest in going out with you or watching a Netflix series which was your favorite activity to do together. More than usual, they are getting out of plans you had agreed upon earlier. They are making excuses to not meet you or ignoring your calls incessantly for no real fault of your own. You must give them the benefit of the doubt in this situation; however, if it is repetitive and it seems as if they are blowing you off, there is a possibility of a third person in the relationship.

Your partner has stopped wearing an engagement ring or may take it off more often. This is a passive sign which you shouldn't concern yourself with a lot. However, if it is happening in addition to other odd changes, then you can be more skeptical. Keep an eye out for the pattern of them not wearing the ring - whether they have casually opted out of wearing it or they remove it when they go out with their friends or at work. If your friends also feel any changes in your relationship and they show concerns about your behavior with each other, it can be a sign. Pay attention to what they are pointing at.

There may be a vivid change in their behavior or habits; for example, you may observe a new way of talking or use of certain words that they never used before. They may start listening to a different type of music. Unlike before, they are coming back home later and their breath smells of alcohol, or they may smell of an unfamiliar scent. They may turn to take a shower immediately after returning from work unless they work at a construction site or workplace of that nature. These are not evident indicators of your partner having an affinity towards someone else, but a person of routine may raise red flags if there is a sudden change in their behavior or habits. They may have suddenly shown an interest in joining a beginner's class or may pursue some activity or hobby which they haven't been interested in before. You may hear them change their stance about politics or any other matter which they were rigid about in the past. They may start talking about movies, series or anything entertaining that is unlike their taste. A person can usually pick up some hobby and there is nothing peculiar about it. However, if it seems inappropriate or odd to their being and they aren't able to justify the reasons properly, there may be a chance of someone else involved. People in long term relationships tend to be aware of routine affairs and any such activity can ring cheating bells in your mind. Be patient before jumping to conclusions, though.

There are unexplained expenses on your spouse's account, or they may ask you to open separate bank accounts. There can be different variations of this. Be on the lookout for unusual bank transactions. Observe if they are visiting the ATM too often, and don't hold back if you have doubts or their activities seem sneaky. You may find them buying new clothes or having other extravagant expenses. Look for any hotel bookings or recurring deposits to an unknown account. Don't ignore if you see new and expensive things that they own and can't explain the nature or the source of them. Illicit financial transactions are a portent of something sneaky happening in a relationship and can be very tricky to deal with. It is best to deal with such situations and provide the supposed unfaithful the bandwidth to either give the benefit of the doubt or to conceal the truth and investigate without tipping off the other person.

They may start talking about friends they have never had before or you may have never heard of, and they suddenly start hanging out with someone you aren't comfortable around. This may simply be a way of getting some time away from you. They may take unexplained trips for the sake of business or with friends and don't seem keen to share exact details with you. They may start "working late" and even go to "work" on weekends. They may refuse to meet friends who have high moral grounds.

They start blaming you for everything wrong in your relationship. They refuse to assume responsibility for anything. They seem to forget things they said previously or just tend to get forgetful about things. A major sign is if they don't want to engage with you sexually. Try to figure out the reason for sex deterioration in the relationship or look out for any changes in their sex habits. This can be a sign or the reason why the relationship is faltering. If the couple is not open about their sexual needs to one another or one doesn't deliver, they may easily fall out of love and look for someone better suited for them. Neither men nor women hold back in seeking what they wish out of a person. Sex deterioration is a part of every marriage. After a couple has kids or is coiling in the complexities of life, it is not easy to keep the same level of prowess in the bed. But the couple can drift apart and if there is no love felt or left, the other person can be drawn to someone else who is ready to provide them with everything missing in their life. It won't be wrong to say you or your partner are a closed book about your sexuality; differences will grow and the relationship will be more likely to fail.

There is a difference in the way they meet you now compared to before. They don't look in your eyes while talking to you and don't kiss you before they leave for work or do any other routine habits they used to do. They may stop giving you compliments. They may accuse you of invading their personal space and guilt you into believing they aren't doing anything wrong. They take more care of their appearance devoid of constant fights and lack of affection from each other. On the contrary, your spouse may become very attentive towards you or may make uncommon gestures. This may be flattering, but make sure this is not overcompensation or a cover-up for something wrong.

They may start shrugging off responsibilities by distancing themselves from their children or other family members. They may refuse to pick your children up from school or accompanying them to classes, not attend their school meetings or refrain from spending extra time with them. Your child may start to feel ignored and unloved. Along with being irresponsible, you may notice a shift in their attitude towards spiritual matters. They may start to defend people who cheat. They may avoid attending church services or behave differently in front of a morally correct individual who can be a friend or a family member.

If your goal is to have a successful and healthy connection, you should be able to trust your partner for letting them into your heart. Surely, you know your partner inside out. You know how he reacts when he is happy, angry, stressed, tired or bored. However, one of the most prominent characteristics of a man who is cheating is when he acts out of character. Their typical behavior, routine and actions begin to change. For example, the amount of time he is spending in the bathroom has increased. There may be subtle changes. Earlier he would watch the football match in the drawing-room, and now he watches them locked in his room. These nuances tend to be wake up calls and need more attention.

Ask yourself if something is wrong if your man suddenly starts to worry about his looks when he couldn't care less about them before. If he starts to buy expensive clothes, wears high end cologne, starts working out or gets too keen to be in shape, when such thoughts haven't even passed his mind in the past. When a man becomes suddenly obsessed with his looks, this shift in his personality can show that he is playing the field.

It is a fact that over 66% of men are guilty of cheating. So, he may try to assuage you and catch you in praise and flattery. Another powerful indicator of your man cheating is if he pulls away all of a sudden. When men cheat, they put all their attention and focus elsewhere. They become less interested and invested in your well-being and events in your life as a couple. If he is acting distant

all of a sudden, it's not a far-off possibility that he is cheating on you.

If he has been a cheater in the past, he is likely to be a cheater. There are two kinds of cheaters. The first type is the people who feel extremely bad about cheating and the second type is the narcissistic kind of cheater. If your man belongs to the second type, don't be surprised if he cheats on you. It's in his nature to cheat and he can't stay loyal to you. The first type is circumstantial. It has been found that even when some men are in fulfilling relationships, they still have a proclivity to cheat. So, if your fulfilling and intimate time together as a couple has reduced significantly or it seems all rushed, distracted and uninterested, he may be sowing his wild oats somewhere else.

He may be quintessentially lying to you. It is a common characteristic of a cheating man. He may lie about where he is, with whom he is, where he is spending his money or who he is calling or texting. Liars tend to repeat what they are saying as if it is rehearsed, or give a lot of unnecessary details while talking. They seem to touch or cover their mouth, fidget or shake nervously, signaling that they are probably holding something back.

Another major indicator of cheating men is they say the wrong name. It's not uncommon that the name of the person who he is cheating with ends up popping out of his mouth, sometimes even at inappropriate times. He may suddenly have a new need for privacy. This is because when he cheats it is an important part of keeping the illusion of his innocence. Keep an eye on his company. The quality of his friends and colleagues influence him the most. Usually, a person who cheats typically hangs out with other men who cheat. Over 80% of cheating men are friends with someone who cheats too.

An almost definite sign that a woman is cheating that you should not ignore is when she starts talking about someone who she works with or some friend more than usual. At that point, she might not be cheating on you with that guy, but she is thinking about him. This may or may not develop into a deep connection. If she doesn't show any interest in your problems or triumphs anymore, she is most likely to be cheating. This is because women are naturally caring, so if she acts absolved of all sensitivity towards you, she is not that into you anymore. She might go missing for a long time. Being aware of her usual whereabouts, if she makes a plan to meet people you have never heard of or she is unable to explain who she spent time with, she is likely to be cheating on you.

She may start working later than her normal hours. This should raise suspicion if you know she is not that into her work. If she starts assuming the time you will meet her or obsessively asks about the time when you will be back home, it is surely a sign. She accuses you of cheating. This is called formatting reaction. The motive is to divulge the blame on the other person because of guilt or regret.

Chapter 6: How to face a betrayal

Being betrayed is one of the worst nightmares for anyone. The consequences can be devastating. Your whole belief system shakes at first glance. Various emotions surface and involuntary thoughts begin to haunt your mind. It is a question that pervades the betrayed: "but why." Often it happens to be preceded by suspicions. Even if one happens to be aware and prepared to face the devil, the trauma is always very strong. It hits like a hurricane when you see the person you invested in agreeing to the fact that they cheated you. You have a mixture of highly explosive feelings, and you continually think, leaving a deep wound in your soul. Try not to be overwhelmed by post-traumatic stress. One loses their sleep, finds it difficult to concentrate, loses weight and can be pushed to the extreme, such as suffering depression or life-ending thoughts. In an ideal world, not a single person would like to deal with the heartbreak that comes after being cheated on. However, it is a harsh reality. Open and honest conversations must precede the need for seeking out an extramarital affair.

When we pick a person and attach ourselves with them, they may choose to stay in unhealthy relationships even where there are problems. If there is secretive behavior on the part of the partner, the person who is cheated on suffers from attachment distress on a very primal level. The moment the person is aware of the betrayal, the distress is profound. Some people fall on to their knees, cry for hours and think about why they even care and why it is so dramatic for them, when they hear about the betrayal for the first time. The initial reaction can also take a route of running away from the shock and shutting yourself down, deciding not to acknowledge the overbearing unfaithful who is belittling the problem and calling it a misunderstanding or plain overreaction from your end. As an unfaithful person, the reveal can end up with them dealing with either a fight, freeze or flight from their partner. Both the unfaithful and the betrayed experience grief, confusion and gush of emotions that need to be dealt with. The more attached the couple is, the greater the extent of grief. It is riveting to feel that after being betrayed, they are exposed to the world. Denial, anger, bargaining, moments of acceptance are cycling in the mind of the betrayed. Bargaining refers to oscillating thoughts of 'what-ifs'. If I lose weight and get attractive, maybe he will come back. If we go for counseling, everything will be okay. The unfaithful may go through the feeling of loss as well. On experiencing their partner acting out, they may immediately think that the relationship is all over and is irretrievable.

When the unfaithful experiences their partner leaning into the situation after finding out the truth, they may find out the betrayed has become highly vigilant. They begin to question everything and yearn for safety. They may become reactive to perceived abandonment.

They will be hypersensitive about any further conversation with their cheating partner. They might stick to little nuances and feel more abandoned and distressed.

When faced with more information, it may crush them, or it may even make them act up or not react at all in a span of ten to twenty minutes. The response to every minute detail can be extreme, or a piece of huge information can derive no reaction out of the sufferer. At this moment, the unfaithful, having caused a lot of atrocity to the betrayed, should feel the need to be available for the other person's acting out, distress and unpredictability. They need to be valiant to make the betrayed feel safe in those moments of primal panic. It is important to bear in mind that at the moment, the person is experiencing a break-in safety. It is irrelevant if it is real or perceived. There is no need to preach to them about what is real and what is perceived. It is a biological response and can't be treated with rationalizing, at least at that very second. Your next thought must be how you can help them. Do your best to not get defensive. Own up to your mistakes. This is very hard to do since the other person may be fighting and our natural response to a fight is defense. Try to just care for them. There should be a questioning process between the aching partner and the unfaithful to understand their feelings better. The thought of making an effort to maximize their comfort should be a priority. Just be there, sit with them and assist them in their pain.

Another response at that moment can be running away after encountering the situation. It may be physical disappearance or emotional leaving, where the person completely shuts down in front of you. Immediately, the hurt may think of hurting and betraying the unfaithful. This spur of giving it back to their cheating spouse is almost involuntary. The unfaithful may jump to conclude that their relationship has come to an end. They may perceive it as the ultimate sign that their partner is going to flee and is easily going to move on, whereas this can just be a mechanism of coping with the trauma by the hurt. It is safety-seeking behavior. They are just dealing with the distress of the situation. The pendulum of emotions where they want to get intimate one day and the next day they want to end the relationship and take their kids away from the betraying partner— these are all reactions caused by the adrenaline rush in different courses of time.

Shifting the focus to what the betrayed can do after encountering a cheating partner will let your emotions cloud you. It is completely natural to be confused. However, bring yourself out of the numbness and experience these feelings. Don't subdue anything you feel. Allowing an emotional build-up will not benefit you in any way. Journal or write about what you are experiencing. Take some time out. Enter your own space. Try to avoid anything that reminds you of the person. If you are living together, it will be best to move out for some time. If you are in a long-term relationship, don't talk to the unfaithful. You may want to steer clear of social media. Try to avoid stalking them or going through your pictures together and just try to keep your mind off it. Refrain from doing something extreme. Getting a makeover or joining the gym to get in shape is normal. Try not to bad mouth your partner, create a scene in the family or file for divorce as an initial reaction. This impulse may lead you to regret later. This should not be misinterpreted as an insinuation of acceptance or forgiveness. These matters should be well thought of for ensuring the safety of the betrayed more than the cheating partner. There is no such thing as absolute revenge. Revenge may just temporarily heal you. It causes more harm than good. The real revenge is soaking the situation in and making the other person repent on their own. There is no better satisfaction than the satisfaction of being in the right.

Seek professional help to deal with the pain. It is impossible to get over the pain and distress caused by your loved one in a day. You can rely on a friend or your parents, or if you don't feel comfortable to have your life discussed, visit a psychiatrist. Speak your heart out and start your healing process. Think about getting better. Try to avoid negative thoughts, and most importantly steer clear of anything that reminds you about them. It is hard to do but it is necessary. Cry it out, act on it, indulge in going out with your friends, stay out for late hours, party hard, plan a vacation, and buy something you wished to but were holding back. The whole point is to make sure you heal your soul and spirit with the least damage done to your wellbeing. Don't correspond with their family members or any of their close friends. Take enough time before you are ready to meet the person again. Confront them bravely. Be strong-headed when you meet them and don't go back into the maze of feeling lost and uncertain. Reflect on what went wrong. At this point, when you have had time to heal, dig up the reason for ending up in this situation. Think about your future. Worry about your kids. It may even involve you getting on your feet again. Don't look for someone else immediately. It is acceptable to sulk and to make people around you feel your pain. It's more about having an outlet for your feelings. But once you are past that, jump on to move ahead in life. You can get in touch with someone who is suffering from a similar heartbreak. You must try to find an opportunity at such times to improve and grow past the situation.

If it is too hard to come to terms with the situation, rather than moving towards something devastating, try to understand what made the relationship falter. Unless you were in a dead-end relationship with a person who is patterned to be a cheater; then that one is on you. The focal point should be rewinding and looking for signs and causes that you think led to the betrayal. It is seldom a one-way stream. Both people in a relationship have failed to fulfill some need of the other person. Be hopeful that the relationship can be saved, even though it seems distant right now. In the chaos, don't ignore the behavior of your partner at this time. The hard part of facing your partner and having a conversation with them is ineludible. You need to hold conversations with your partner to know if they intend to save the marriage. Where do you both stand after facing the blow of infidelity? Are you both keen on breaking the relationship? If not, then what's holding you back? What specifics of the affair do you need to know about? Why did your partner need this other person? Where did they meet them? Before venturing into the physicality of their illicit relationship, you may need to consult a psychiatrist or a trusted friend or your family beforehand. Now take time to evaluate and reach a certain point of view. See if they are sorry, remorseful or disinterested. Talk about you and your partner's conversation with someone you trust.

Sometimes the betrayed experiences a rage due to a pressing need to talk about the extent the unfaithful partner went to, and they refuse to provide details or may not care to make amends. If you wonder why they don't fully provide you the details you want them to reveal, don't take this the hard way and don't indulge in self-doubt. For the unfaithful to withhold the information is the most selfish thing that they can do at this moment. It's enough that they have ripped their partner's heart out and yet refuse to provide them with what they deserve to know. To not provide them the information is similar to leaving someone to solve a jigsaw puzzle in darkness. The cheating partner is most likely to be too ashamed or the details are too painful to discuss, and they might feel you won't be able to handle it. When the betrayed person tries to put all the pieces together, they aren't trying to shame you. They are just trying to put all the pieces together. An unfaithful person doesn't particularly enjoy talking about his affair, addiction, choices and pain because it is uncomfortable. However, the betrayed spouse cannot heal without being able to talk about what has happened. If they don't get this information, they may get infuriated. Their imagination can go wild and they may start to imagine what happened and what did not happen. They try to put together different scenes and imagine the worst, and ultimately their pain compounds. They are unaware about what to forgive. They remain in a state of paralysis. Most probably, the unfaithful can't talk about it because they are not healed. When shame is triggered, people usually shut down and it may seem impossible for them to bring their disloyalty out in the open. The unfaithful may fear to relive their mistakes more than the betrayed wanting to hear the information, hence the silence.

Another reason why they must be holding back is probably because there may be more to the story that what they previously admitted to. They feel they will lose a chance of any kind of restoration if they reveal all the missing pieces. To avoid the situation, the betrayed must ensure them that they will digest all the information and wait before jumping to any conclusions. This may be stoically agonizing to do, but if you want to have full disclosure, this is something that you must agree to do.

Chapter 7: Consequences of a betrayal on children

It is in no way questionable that in a failing relationship, the biggest impact falls on the children. Children love their parents, and in every household, parents are their role models. Comparatively, children these days are closer to their parents while growing up than kids who were born in the 1980s or 1990s. Parents should assume responsibility in looking after their children by keeping their personal battles aside, since any fall out in their upbringing can change their lives for the worse. It is really important to see a failed relationship from the eyes of adolescents and young adults. Here is an instance of the impact on a client's child while getting counseled. "My parents are divorced and all my friends at school think I'm funny, crazy and happy all the time, but when I get home and go to bed, I just lay there and cry for a long period, but no one knows about it. I live with my father, my three sisters and my mother lives in a different country. I love both my parents equally. I only get to see my mother in the holidays, and I miss her a lot." He is thirteen years old and his parents split up when he was four.

The impact that the split of parents has on children depends on a host of complex circumstances and situations. Some children turn out to be great if removed from conflicted environments, whereas some may not, or some may stay unaffected no matter what. However, the split does have a short-term impact on children. Many suffer from lower self-esteem, anxiety, depression, poor-quality contact with their parents and their standard of living decreases. These impacts linger into adulthood to have long-term impacts. Children may continue to have psychological difficulties or not have very comfortable relationships with their parents. Most of them may end up getting divorced themselves or experience non-functional relationships influenced by their parents.

Failed relationships carve the path to a disloyal future for children. It is true that a lot of children who are raised by parents who have drifted apart due to cheating end up being unfaithful in their relationships. Parent's behavior shapes their mind. If one of the parents they are close to ends up cheating, this may cause them to think of it as acceptable behavior, and they may repeat that in their relationships in the future. Betrayal between their parents can affect their psychology, making them confused since they are too young to understand. In contrast, a young adult may show aversion towards the cheating parent altogether and their whole support system shakes. No one is born with the ability to understand a betrayer and the children may reason it to be their fault.

Alternatively, kids may seem to be ashamed of the cheating parent and may get talked about at school. Other than their parents, they are the most affected by their friends. If the lives of their parents are discussed, it makes them feel exposed. Pent-up feelings back home and open discussions about their personal lives, which may get indecent, can adversely affect children. This gives rise to anxiety, nervous pressures, and low self-esteem. They may look for someone they can rely on and if there is a toxic environment at home and difficult environment in their school or college, they may start to act up or shut down their feelings.

When children have a falling out with their close friends, they learn to get past it. There are various issues, especially in this day and age as kids are exposed to a worldwide network, that they need their parents to guide them through more than ever. Children can be mean to each other and sometimes a social media post is enough to push them over the edge. This can lead to your kid overcoming the chaos and focusing on studies or other useful things.

Children may suffer from abandonment issues and act possessive and develop into insecure individuals as they grow up. The fact that they are living with a single parent or living with their stepparents can make them ache for the other parent's presence. Their fear of losing the other parent also thrives and puts a burden on everyone who later forms a friendship or relationship with them. They stop believing in love and weigh in a lot before opening up to someone. They find it extremely difficult to trust anyone. They may refuse to give any benefit of the doubt to their partners, correlating it all to their parent's relationship.

It has been proven how children are affected by their parent's relationship depending on the degree of the parent's conflict and how caught up they are in it. For example, if parents are fighting and the father asks his son to tell his mother that he won't be able to attend his parent's day at school. The mother responds to him through the son, asking why would he pass this message through him and not directly talk to her. This is when the child gets meddled in the fight and becomes a part of the conflict. This stresses them. They may even feel forced to take sides with one and lose connection with the other. For children, both parents are equally important and dear to them. They may also think that they are a reason for these constant fights between their parents and resort to self-harm.

Their trouble begins when they see their parents fight, and continues through the splitting up process and goes further along after that. It is hard when these days, divorce has become so common and so many kids are dealing with it. In each stage of the process, kids are impacted differently and they need to receive equal love and attention from both parents even if they decide to co-parent or not. Otherwise, pangs of separation will scar them for life. If parents are constantly fighting and there is a poor communication and support system in the house, children can still develop these issues. Parents need to realize that their children are a priority. They need to be sensitive to their needs and have an open conversation about their issues. They must try to avoid fighting around them and making them a part of their fights. Children should be left to worry about their school and studies rather than getting caught up in misunderstandings at home. The rules to co-parent must be as child-friendly as possible. One must not bad mouth the other person in front of them. The rest of the family members must also show the same love and care towards them, despite the failed relationship between their parents. Keep your arguments away from the children and raise them in a healthy and sustainable environment. Be available to answer their doubts and inhibitions. Try to obtain their validation every step of the way and explain to them suitably about what is going on around them. Share every piece of information and note their behavior around you closely. Keep in touch with their close friends' parents.

Look after your children's bodies. Their bodies tell a lot about what they are feeling. Keep an eye on their eating habits. If they complain about continuous stomachaches, they may be feeling pent-up emotions and not be able to digest their food properly. An obvious reaction when a child is around his parent fighting is their heart rate increasing. They may feel faint and scared. Excess stress hormones may get released, which are very bad for their growth and overall health.

If either of the child's parents is emotionally unavailable, the child goes through a tough time. If you are an emotionally distant father, your child may lift that baggage and put it in his new relationships. He needs to heal and for this, he first needs to be aware of what kind of father he has. The father can be disapproving, mentally ill, substance-abusing, abusive, and unreliable or absent. He can be one or a combination of these traits. He should carefully note which one represents his relationship with his father. It is necessary to recall how he was treated by him as a child. He can journal his feelings, talk to his siblings or his other parent. This is necessary to stop any teasing or trauma from developing or to remove an already existing one. It may be painful so it will be better for him to do this in therapy if possible. Look for the coping mechanisms he used or uses to get his father's attention. Consider which of these mechanisms are still active today. See if these are acting up to stop him from being entirely happy. Maybe he is still a workaholic or tries to go unnoticed in any situation. Think of some new ways and behavioral changes that will help him to lead a better life and accept the situation better. For example, eating disorders would have helped him get through some tough times earlier, but now it's better to get past self-harming ways and live the life he deserves to live.

If the child had an abusive, emotionally distant or a mean mother, there are ways to heal and feel fully accepted, comforted and understood. Maybe she doesn't stay with him anymore or she has not been very receptive towards him. The truth about healing from an emotionally distant mother is that it has a lot to do with attachment. Attachment is so important for every child because it lays a safe foundation. It makes the child feel safe to go into the world and do things that seem too hard to do on his own. Not having this foundation can make you turn cold and you may find it difficult to show empathy or soothing emotions towards another person. He may become unable to express himself and when he notices someone else expressing their feelings to him, he wouldn't know how to be comforting. So, it decreases his comfort levels around anything which is emotionally driven.

There is a child's voice which is innately present in everyone. His emotions are stuffed up because he doesn't feel safe expressing them. This child's voice remains suppressed over all these years. So, it is necessary for him to find that inner voice and express everything he means to say. He can pen it down and it will be like a written letter from a child-like self to an adult self. Everything hurtful that happened, all the feelings you had that you couldn't express or tantrum you couldn't throw. Just anything that is pent-up and needs to be released from inside you. A therapy session like a safe space to do this can be so incredibly healing. He may miss a rub on the back, a warm hug or comfort of a mother's company. They can work on good mother messages that you always wanted to hear from your mother. It could be like 'I love you no matter what', 'You are so amazing' and 'I am always here for you' while doing something caring for himself. It can seem odd or even creepy, but this will make him feel a lot better in building up his support. He can visit an attachment-based trauma specialist because they can help him deal with these issues and turn them into something healthy for him. With that said, the right way to foster healing is for the child to work on his relationship with himself rather than with anyone else. Engage in worrying about his well-being and trying to grow and make the best out of any situation thrown his way.

Chapter 8: After the storm the calm

After the betrayal unfolds, the relationship may end and both partners may decide to take different paths. They may also insist on staying friends, but in such cases, the relationship had seen the last of it and the betrayal was the end chapter that sealed the closing of the book. As the story ends, it is important to face and accept the situation. Sometimes, ending the relationship is the best solution for both parties. The aftermath of those devastating moments of learning about the betrayal can be manifold. Concerns arising may be about finance or a shaken support system, and one of the most important decisions is choosing whether to leave or stay. The question you need to find answers to is if the relationship you are trying to save is the right one for you. Can you be happy in the relationship? Despite the current situation, do you still feel in your heart that you can take the person back? If you don't know the answers to this question, the relationship and your current situation will not be fixable. You will have problems and regret. The regret can be about either leaving them when it could have been saved, or regret can be about sticking with them or emotionally challenging yourself to ultimately conclude that it can't work out anymore.

How do you know if your relationship is worth it? And before that, why do you want to be in the right relationship? This comes down to the real purpose of your life. Most would agree that the purpose of life is to be happy. Your relationship paves the path to your happiness. It exists because it makes you happy. Your relationship meets your needs and helps to bring out the best in you. If you are not in the right relationship, then you won't be able to be content. You won't be able to achieve your full God-given potential. Life will seem to be harder and you will always feel short of experiencing true love and well-roundedness of wellbeing.

Unfulfilling relationships can lead to bad examples for your children. Therefore, it is vital to your happiness and fulfillment.

While evaluating if you are in the right relationship, it is exigent to weigh in relationship problems. These problems are catalysts that are causing emotional stress, doubts and confusion, which may take away from what the other person means to you. You must begin by being honest to yourself. Know thyself. Be self aware and just make an effort to know what you need in life or any relationship or situation. Everything comes back to knowing yourself. It's not about material things that you wish to own. These things provide momentary happiness. You need to be aware of the feelings you need. How do you want to feel day-to-day and on a moment-by-moment basis? The questions you need to ask yourself for finding out what you need are what feelings are important to you. Here are some examples: happiness, security, peace, passion, intimacy, adventure, love, freedom. Think about what matters to you the most. And try to put it in one sentence about what you want to attain in your life. In other words, when you lie on your deathbed, what do you want people surrounding you to say about you? What do you want your life to have meant in the eyes of your loved ones and yourself? The next thing is to name three things that you currently want to do that will make you happy. These can be activities or anything you are involved in or affected by. Lastly, what do you think is an ideal lifestyle for you? How would you want to live ideally? It can be very different for every person. You may wish to have a penthouse in the countryside and live a simple life, being one with nature, or you may desire to travel around the world. Pen down if you want to own a house or really just take care of your pets. These are some diverse examples of what ideal living means to you. When you answer all these questions you will know what you yearn for in your life.

The next step is to find your ideal partner. Think that you can step out of your current situation and enter a theoretic and ideal world. You may or may not include your current spouse in this. Paint a picture in your mind about what you feel makes your marriage fitting in making you genuinely happy. Don't put any restrictions on yourself. The picture should be about what you and your partner should be doing together and what feelings would you and your ideal partner be giving to each other. This can be very different. Some can imagine backpacking across South America where some may wish to build a business together, or some may live far off in the countryside. The following step involves you to partner match. You start to match up the current partner with your ideal partner. This is going to give you an idea of whether your current partner is perfect for you or not. You can move to imagine their ideal lifestyle and compare it to yours and notice the overlap. Are you wanting the same things, and more importantly, the same feelings? Certain people in relationships want different things out of their marriage, so it's important to see if there are any red flags. You need to see if your desires and aspirations are so drastically different than your partner's that it would be difficult for you to accommodate each other's needs. Usually, this mismatch causes major relationship problems such as lack of intimacy, arguments and fights. It is ultimately necessary to be accepting of your partner's needs.

If the two of you want different things, then there must be room for personal space and flexibility between them. There must be a drive to go the extra mile and compromise to reach each other's ultimate goals and create a strong, reliable future together. These feelings may change from time to time, so it's necessary to be in constant talks about feelings at various stages in the relationship. Identify what got both of you together in the first place. The question to face here is if you were really in love. Have you ever been in love? To generalize a few points - love is not all about chemistry or lust or initial attraction. These things change over time. You can't equate love to lust. Love is the ability to make each other feel good and this comes through shared values. You may describe or rewind the memories of the first meeting and enunciating the feelings you felt at the time you two got together. Recount all the events, not to describe them to someone else, but really for yourself to evaluate what led you to come together in the first place. Then, check whether the highest values at the time for you matched that of your partner's. See if you both were looking for the same feelings. Think about your doubts, uneasy feelings or fears before entering the relationship. If so, then what were those thoughts, and do you still think they are relevant? It is not uncommon to have these feelings. It's necessary to be aware of such feelings. Try to note down what is the number one reason for you getting into a relationship with this person.

Now, you have to get to the current situation. You have to evaluate what feelings you have about your spouse currently. What is the real cause of all the problems between you? Are the problems clouding your true feelings for your partner? You can do this by first writing about all the things you like about your partner's personality. Identify things you like about them and things that you wish to change. After preparing a list, you need to evaluate how important it is for you to change this personality trait. Find how much trouble it causes you and rate it on a scale of one to ten. They don't need to change for you, but you feel it is vital for you to maintain your sanity. The next step is to check how difficult it will be for your partner to change it. Since you desperately want them to change, rate this difficulty faced by them. These steps will let you understand how you feel and how your spouse feels about you and your relationship. It is also a kind of reality check about how compatible you are. Lastly, you need to ask yourself the reason for being in the relationship. What is the driving force? It can either be negative or positive. Try to think about the good reasons for being in the relationship. You need to think about their good qualities and relive the good times. Think about the best qualities of your partner and see if that makes you smile internally. Acknowledge the surge or the flutter in your heart and good times you have had together. Negative reasons for staying in the relationship can be fear. You may have fears that are holding you back. Experiencing guilt, loss of face or worrying about what your family, friends or your children will think if you left, or there could be financial reasons. It could be because you don't want your kids to be raised in a broken home, or it could be cultural or religious reasons that forbid you to leave the person you are committed to, and the most important fear of all is the fear of actually being alone and not being loved. By now, working on all these points, you must have clearly understood your feelings.

On clearly knowing about your feelings, you become more alive and energized. The energy around you takes a shift. After going through life aimlessly or being worried about your problems all the time, you obtain direction. There is almost something very distinctive about such people. They seem to be always on fire. They have a magnetic quality about them and seem to be radiant. It is a personally driven directive which makes them very compelling and confident. Usually, when a marriage or a relationship is faltering, people may feel that they have fallen out of love. Suddenly, they stop feeling happy and they reason it's the marriage and their partner not being able to make them happy. They lose interest in them and confuse it as a lost connection. At this moment, you feel that leaving your partner will make you happy. However, the fact is that the failing relationship is only a symptom of the problem of not having or knowing your real purpose in life. If the person finds out what they are here for and what they are supposed to be doing, she/he will feel better about her/his life and ultimately perceive their marriage as useful. When you are not in an inspiring place in your relationship or your life, the common symptoms make you feel that your growth has stopped. But when you are working towards your purpose, you are on the verge of the steepest trajectory and at the edge of growth. In relationships where love or attraction goes stale, usually, it is because the evolutionary edge has stopped. What compels us into relationships, marriage or business is the purpose. The ignition or raw passion in the beginning always fades away, and it can reach the point of feeling like a burden or prison. There is a parallel between the raw senses of passion in the start, also known as the honeymoon phase. Losing interest and that passion is the decline stage, where there is no inspiration. The whole relationship seems to diffuse. So, to stop that from happening, you need to divert your attention to how you are feeling currently and bring changes in your life accordingly to stay interested and focused, and not get caught in the rut of the cycle of life.

A lot of people have growth as their forefront goal in life, while others may seek security. People in a relationship fail to realize that they are changing. When it reaches a stable point in terms of growth and development in their life, they suddenly find that it's not providing them fulfillment. So, whatever gave us fulfillment early on, we stop doing that and we go on without anticipating what was working. As a child learns about something, they find it extremely interesting and curious. After mastering and acquiring all the knowledge that they needed to, they move on to learning newer things. Similarly, in a relationship, there has to be something that reignites the feelings and brings you back in terms of what made you start the relationship. What was once a fresh fertile soil has now become a whole landscape that has turned stale. If you need to reinvigorate, you have to reconnect with the newness.

    Sex has an important part to play in this. Sex in the relationship can't be perceived as something to be done twice a week in the same way for fifty years and never getting bored with it. Doing this whole thing of finding new ways to make a relationship exciting and doing new things together can't be easily done, no matter how well you know the other person. In a healthy relationship, both of you are changing and the whole dynamic keeps changing. It takes a lot of effort and focus to keep the momentum going. There is, for instance, a large number of people who change their jobs multiple times before they take a steady job. There is a rapid change that goes on. It is a metamorphic phenomenon and this centers around our mastery on each level of the game. Things may start to lose their edge a little. But then new edges appear, and growth continues. When you retrospectively map someone's career, you notice that due to some reason they stopped and moved on to the next best option. This is real progression, and just how it's applied in our lives everyday, you shouldn't refrain from doing the same in your relationships. You need to sharpen your awareness to follow this thread. This also casts light on pressures put on people from society. The instant gratification that you will be happier if you get this or that, or perhaps moving in the same direction as others are moving in. The whole cycle of ego and wishing life speeds up is quickening. We are always in an unprecedented territory because all the rules about relationships no longer seem to apply, and we have much higher expectations about what we want from our relationship.

We want the higher things from relationships, so once these emotional needs are met—especially if continually—we start to question things. If you are being divorced or you are trying to pull away from a person, there is nothing more important for you to do than to know your purpose. Purpose makes you attractive. Hartville Hendricks described something called the isolate fuser dynamic. The isolator fuse dynamic entails one person doing the running and the other person doing the chasing. The isolator unconsciously pushes others away and keeps people at a distance because they need a lot of space around them. Freedom is very important to them. The fuser is the one who has an insatiable need for closeness. Fusers want to do things together all the time. If people fail to meet them on time, they start to feel abandoned. The thought of divorce makes them cry. They crave physical affection and reassurance, and they need to stand in close verbal contact. Sometimes, they may switch roles. There is a lot of flexibility derived from just calling yourself a fuser type or isolate type. Various relationships can bring out these specific aspects of ourselves. The fuser energy is more aligned with feminine energy inside the system, and isolate is mostly aligned with the masculine. Though all of us have both. But the two are very different drivers. The core principle behind feminine energy is love. Females could remain largely unfulfilled until this energy comes to know itself as love. For the masculine principle, which is internally embedded in us, the primary energy behind it is purpose. The purpose is greater than itself and it remains unfulfilled unless it is ignited by another purpose.

When you have someone in your life playing the fuser role, they are a little more oriented in the love or heart space, whereas the isolate partner is out in the world and their focus is on the partner or career or business or just anything. The fuser needs to get aligned with a purpose. The part of what makes the isolate so attractive is their attention is not on the fuser. They are aligned with their things. It is carved off and making them unavailable. This is exactly what the fuser needs to be doing. To get connected with yourself to achieve this, you need to do several things. Recognize yourself in that fuser role where you are the one who is chasing, and your partner is running. Their attention is not on you or your family. There is something that they are compelled to do, which is the other person. You realize the attention is going elsewhere. Getting in touch with the isolator quality will provide you strength. Your sense of self will get stronger and less reliant on your isolator. You will feel like a brick around them as opposed to feeling like a wreck. The effect of the way they are treating you won't affect you as much, and you may experience a backbone building that will aid you in standing alone. Your partner is going to experience this shift, and this may make them wish to come back in and reconnect. Therefore, it is critical to have a purpose.

If you are putting a lot of effort to get back with the person and you are doing everything you can to keep the relationship together and the other person is just not responding, and they are still insisting on leaving you, or they are still ignoring you or treating you badly, they may be refusing communication. Alternatively, they could even be carrying on with an affair which can be either emotional or physical. If you are in this situation, it is very easy to be despondent and disheartened and even more upset with the whole situation. The whole thing doesn't seem fair. It may seem like you are making all the effort and the other person is carrying on without any sign of consideration for you. There are a few things that you can do in this situation. The first thing to realize is that if you have a spouse who wants to go away and you want to stay together, you are facing one of the most difficult situations you could ever face. You both want different things right now. As you both moved forward in your relationship since the inception, things have changed. We may sometimes forget about this, but change is a fact of life. So, your spouse has changed, and the situation of your relationship has changed. Sometimes conflicts arise in the relationship and we resist to change according to the circumstances. This resistance may have been caused by not accepting the changes. We may look back and feel things were better than they probably were. But we find it difficult to accept that things are different. So, the first step is to accept that both you and your partner have changed, and there is nothing wrong with that. It is perfectly natural. You need to take away the expectation that they should want to stay married to you. When you put pressure on someone, that is the fastest way to drive them away from the relationship. Keep reminding yourself that expectations mean more pressure and that pressure will push your partner farther away. But how can this be done without actually feeling disappointed when they refuse to accommodate your needs? You need to remember how things are going is the best for your marriage. You have feelings and you wish to have a great relationship because you love them. But by making a few changes yourself, you can make them interested in staying with you and rid of the pressures that are pushing them away.

Get rid of the feeling that you need to stay in a relationship or stay married to this person in your life to stay happy. Of course, you want to be together with them and you want to feel all the good things of having them in your life. But it is possible to leave them, say if your life depended on it. It could be possible for you to find someone else to have a happy relationship with. You don't want to do that, but you could if you had to. So, you don't need your spouse to be happy. When you get it, you will be amazed at just how happy you start to feel. Nothing would have changed on the outside. You would still be married, and you might be in the current situation with all the bad parts, but you would have evolved on the inside. The ultimate truth is when things start to change on the inside, they begin to change on the outside. So ultimately, you want to stay together and you want things to work out, but you don't need to be with them. Next, you need to start focusing on yourself. Ask yourself how you can be happy. We often forget when things get out of touch in our relationship, we habit ourselves into remaining upset and try to work hard to fix our problems. We are trying so hard to keep our partner happy that we forget about our own happiness. Don't tell yourself that once your relationship is healed and you both are back together, you will be happy. You need to feel that you don't need the relationship to make you happy. You are enough. Make a list of things that you can do at the moment that will make you happy. Start doing them almost immediately to feel good.

    Don't think that's selfish on your part to do something that's keeping your mood light at this problematic time. Imagine if you ever see your children or someone who you love being happy, would you tell them to stop because they should rather focus on their problems, or would you just be glad to see them happy? Then why not treat yourself with the same love and respect? You deserve to be in a happy place in your life. Another step in the process of healing from your uncooperative partner is to allow them to make mistakes. They might go off to do stupid things. They might have an affair, they may start texting someone something inappropriate, they might yell at you, they might ask for a divorce. They are saying this because everybody makes mistakes, including you. We start expecting them to be perfect and not make any mistakes at all; however, that is not a part of being a human being. Then you need to work on changing the meaning of what's hurting you. If you are feeling hurt, it doesn't necessarily come from someone else or what someone else has done to you. It comes from what you think about that person's actions. It's about what you perceive their actions to mean. You have different expectations about what that person should or shouldn't have done. A person may say that he is hurt because his wife cheated on him and she shouldn't have done that. The wife may respond by saying he should not have been so cold towards her. He should have considered my feelings. But think, why should they consider your emotions? People are truly doing only one thing in their entire life, which is trying to be happy. So instead of reacting, being hurt, saying my husband or wife should make amends, ask yourself a different and much more powerful question—I wonder why they have done it. Is there anything I can do to help? See if you can find a different meaning for your behavior. And lastly, give it some time. Things take time to work and things are going to change. The situation right now is not permanent. They won't continue to act in this way forever. Soon you will have to make a decision—to choose if you want to keep trying or if you have had enough. It is not possible to say in general terms how long it will take for your relationship to get back to normal, or if it will ever reach the point that you both are happy together again. But it's paramount that you value yourself. Work on your own happiness first.

Chapter 9 "What to do to get happy again"

A question that haunts the mind of the betrayed is whether the unfaithful person ever regrets their decision. Whether their partner will ever miss them or just easily move on with someone else after having made them suffer miserably. Usually the betrayed feels like they are the only mourners of the relationship. Society will judge them because everyone will think they could not provide something to the other person. But the unfaithful suffer too. They might not be communicating it, but it is true. The most important thing that the betrayed needs to do to be completely happy again is to let go of the will to seek revenge. You need to understand that your partner is not a sociopath. They may be portraying that they are unaffected, but life has a way of coming full circle. They will have their accountability and suffering that they need to deal with on their end. As this quote by Tim Keller rightly says, "We have to release the urge to exact the payment from the other and make them hurt how we hurt and feel what we feel if we truly want to forgive." Therefore, forgiveness is paramount to the journey. Everyone has their path that they choose for themselves. If someone decides to leave you, it is their choice, even though it is extremely selfish. Yet, if you two stay together, then you both might be miserable.

When you are upset over getting dumped and you beat yourself up for falling for that person, keep breathing. Tolerate the hurt and try to find your new normal self. You are allowed to whine and sulk in front of people who surround you. Focus on your feelings. Attempt to comprehend what it is that hurts the most. If you don't fully know what is causing the hurt, you won't be able to overcome and move on. You may be bent out of shape due to your loss. You don't feel like you are good at getting anything done and the loss has left a mark. You may feel that you are not interested in and capable of finding love again. These feelings make you vulnerable. There is a contradiction in your mind about whether you would have been happy if you were still together with that person. At this moment you might even forget about the abuse and neglect or betrayal that you faced while being in the relationship. The anger about losing your dignity and value hits hard. But it is necessary to acknowledge there is a loss. To enter into the next phase of your life and to be happy, you need to face this loss. Without being aware of it, you can never finish your feelings for them. Therefore, forgiving the person is paramount to a healthy life. The unfaithful have their moments of incredible shame and humiliation too. It is not easy for anyone to get away with their wrongdoings. It comes back to them or it may already be haunting them. Just to not lose face, they may be acting stronger, aloof or unaffected.

One of the prominent differences between being in a happy relationship than in a failing one is how couples deal with mistakes. We all make mistakes. Somehow, we believe that people in perfect marriages or relationships never make mistakes. They don't have any problems. They are different and better people than the rest of us. The truth of the matter is that people who are in great marriages still make a lot of mistakes. They may even make more mistakes, but the real distinguishing factor is in how they deal with them. The meaning they attach to mistakes is different than others. There are certain things that you can do to attach a different meaning to mistakes in your relationship so you can deal with them in a much better way. The quality of your love depends on what you think making a mistake means to you. It is irrespective of how big we feel the mistake is. It could be a major mistake like betraying your partner, but it can also be smaller things that impact your relationship negatively. It could be losing your temper, getting angry and shouting at your spouse, or being cold and non-communicative with them or refusing to consider their feelings. How we look at mistakes can have a very devastating effect. It can cause a lot of stress and strain in the relationship. They keep your relationship stuck in a negative space. Whatever you focus on, you will get more of it. If you focus on trying to get over something or trying to heal from a mistake, you are going to get more and will need to put in more effort and time. It may also drive a person to make more mistakes. Any person who is weak in a relationship is unattractive. If you have made a mistake and you are making an effort to make everything better, you start to feel bad about yourself. You are being weak. You are not going to be attractive to your spouse. If you have made a mistake and are dwelling on it or you are trying to heal yourself or your spouse from it, it is going to have the opposite effect. Reacting to a mistake in the wrong way can offend and create an imbalance in power. If you are the perpetrator and your partner is the victim, it creates inequality between both. It takes the couple away from one place that they want to be in. You both want to be in a happy and easy, fun-loving space in your relationship now. Mistakes are made in the past and if you keep focusing on overcoming them it keeps you in the past. The dictionary definition of a mistake is an error or fault resulting from defective judgment, deficient knowledge or carelessness. Defective means not being perfect.

Everyone most commonly forgets that no one is perfect. Being defective is an integral part of being a human being. It's natural to make mistakes. Then deficient knowledge can be interpreted as mistakes that come from a result of things that we simply don't know. If we don't know how to react in a situation or to a particular event because it might be a new experience, we won't know the right thing to do. No one has perfect knowledge. We can also make mistakes when we are not careful and not paying attention and simply being careless. The consequence of doing something rash like losing your temper or even connecting inappropriately with a third person, like having a physical or emotional affair, is difficult to undo, but our minds can be clouded by our emotions. We are not using our logical mind at this point to make our decisions. There are a few things that do not come under the ambit of the word 'mistake'. First, if a mistake isn't intentional, it isn't something that was done out of spite for our partner. We can't imagine the consequences, so it's not intended. The mistake made is not permanent; it might have been a single incident or could have been repeated multiple times, such as developing a negative attitude towards your spouse. The damage occurs when we stick to it. We realize it's beginning but don't want to see the end of it. We keep the memory of the mistake and that is just internally harming our own heart and soul. So, the mistake has ended but we are stuck in the damage it has caused.

Acknowledge that you have made a mistake, both to yourself and your partner. You don't need to justify yourself or come up with reasons or any long analysis of why you acted the way that you did. Just say it to yourself and to your spouse that you made a mistake and that you are sorry. The next important thing is to stop apologizing. Once is enough. Stop continually reminding the partner that you or they made a mistake by either apologizing or by complaining about it. It won't make any positive difference. It is distracting you from thinking what you are supposed to think and feel at the moment. Stop being responsible for your partner's feelings. The moment anyone takes

responsibility for someone else's feelings, they will never achieve true harmony in the relationship. We need to take full responsibility for our feelings. It takes you away from attaining the basic goal of happiness and fulfillment in your life. It might be hard. They might be angry with you and they could be blaming you and make you feel guilty. They might even threaten your relationship. But it is their problem. You are not going to see any true progress towards creating a really happy marriage until you and your spouse start learning to take responsibility for your feelings. You both are adults, and you both can learn to be more self-aware. So, don't keep taking this responsibility away from them and allow them to learn how to be responsible for their feelings. If that's all that you do in your relationship, it will seem to genuinely transform. Try to see the other side of making mistakes. Just focus on what was the good that the mistake brought to you. What has your mistake or your partner's mistake taught you? How can you use it to improve your relationship? What good things can now happen in the relationship as a result of having made the mistake? Mistakes are small reminders of what is not right between a couple. If you do not take the mistake as a warning and you perhaps carry on doing it, this can have a disastrous effect on your marriage. What is the positive side of having an affair? Probably it has made you realize that you have lost the fun and intimacy in your marriage and you have stopped doing those things together that made the relationship fun, or you have stopped appreciating your husband/wife for the wonderful person they are. It is like a wake-up call. It calls for a lot of awareness and effort to make those things right rather than just letting the marriage or relationship slide away.

You need to create a new meaning for the word mistake. Calling a mistake an error or a fault is quite negative. It sounds like something you are doing wrong. The definition that successful marriages have or some great people have is that a mistake is a learning opportunity and a gift that you have been given to make your life better. If you see your mistakes this way, you will feel there is a huge opportunity to learn and grow and improve your life. It will make you and your partner a better person. Expect to make more mistakes. Look forward to making more mistakes. People who have this mentality see things more positively. It gets wired into your brain. You gleam with positivity since the negative definition of calling a mistake an error is now delightfully called an opportunity to sprout. For instance, Thomas Edison tried multiple times to make a bulb after several attempts. He was asked by reporters if he ever felt discouraged after failing. He said he couldn't imagine it working. The real wonder was when he made the discovery. This attitude of accepting and embracing your flaws can take you places in your relationship and cement the foundation of your relationship, no matter what the mistakes are that plague it. It is not actually what happens that determines how happy you are, but it is about the meaning we attach to the things happening around us. If you change the meaning that you have attached to your partner's past mistakes, you are going to start to act differently. You will get different results.

Can you save your relationship when your partner has already left? Can it be saved if they are seeking a divorce? If you are in a situation where your husband or your wife has packed their bags and moved out and filed for divorce, it is very devastating. It brings a sense of reality to the fact that your marriage really might be over. You may have talked about ending your marriage for weeks or months. You might have tried extremely hard for them to stay by counseling or making amends. It feels like the end of the dreams and memories that you shared and the things in the future that you wanted to share with them as well. You start to make decisions about your life and future. You are single again. Accept where you are right now and how you are taking it. You feel terrible and life looks bleak. It's important not to deny or fight. You are feeling lonely and things aren't good. The next thing to realize is it's never too late to save your marriage. People get together with their partners after weeks, months or even years after being separated. People even get divorced and remarry someone else and then get back together. So, the bottom line is it is never too late to save your marriage or relationship. The reason why you can't save your relationship is that you decide you don't want to save the marriage. As time goes on, you realize you are much happier without that person than you were with them. You are finding you're capable of finding greater happiness with someone else or somewhere else. It is the most important outcome of your life that you are happy. The other reason is that you give up. If your husband/wife loved you once, they can love you again. Even if more people come into their lives and different things happen that upset you, the emotions that your partner felt for you once can be felt again.

Something that you can do to move your partner in your direction, despite them having left you, is to not panic. It is a very hard and stressful time. They have already left your sight. You will need to be in a far stronger place to make things work without giving up and without finding your happiness somewhere else. You will have to make better decisions. Stop looking backwards. If you start to question where you are now by looking back at what went wrong in the relationship, you will be creating negative feelings. You will create blame, shame, guilt, anger, resentment or depression. None of them will help your situation, but rather make things worse. Start looking forward into your future.

This means focus on the future that you want to have. You want to be happily married or stay together with your partner? Thinking about this doesn't help to achieve it. But it does make you positive and hopeful. It sends you to a much better place to get your husband/wife back. Be positive when you are around them. You must be cheerful, upbeat, pleasant and optimistic. It doesn't mean to give them everything they say they want or to become weak. It doesn't mean that you condone or forgive their behavior. It just means that you don't allow any negative feelings or energy to creep into any dealings that you have with them. Your behavior is going to make a big impression on them. The positivity is going to rub off on them and make a big difference. Lastly, you need to pick yourself up and get out of your current situation. Pick up a new hobby and do new things. Surround yourself with people who will make you feel good. Try to take some action to create a positive future. It is very rewarding to take control of your life. With great things happening in your life, you will begin to feel better. You may also start enjoying yourself too much and think that you are happier without being married to your husband/wife. For some people, divorce becomes the best thing that's ever happened to them. They later think about how they ever imagined being happy with that person. If you thought you were happy, now you are realizing the true meaning of being happy. This is not suggesting that you have this outcome, nor should you look at this outcome and judge your situation. But when you focus on your happiness, you are going to start to feel better.

    Who you are is very attractive and when you live by being honest and true to yourself, you become attractive to the world. When the estranged spouse sees you living a happy life they start to find you much more attractive than they ever did. They may start asking themselves what they are missing out on. They may start to miss being a part of your great life. Many people have had very messy divorces and very tragic things happen to them in their lives. But these people would likely agree that the worst things that happened to them, in some ways, actually turned out to be the best thing that could have ever happened to them. Your struggles make you grow and help you get stronger. You start to live through your true self rather than just living a routine. You may struggle with your fears. The better the person you are, the better the life you are going to have. The more you deal with adversity, the better the person you become. You then attract a better life for yourself. So, a lot of it has to do with your mental attitude, your beliefs and strength you build in your mind.

Once you're at a crossroads, you can be in three situations. First is when you forgive your spouse and you are ready to reconcile with them. It's much more likely that you end up back together. You may reconcile but are unable to forgive them. This is the place where you are stuck in negative thoughts and you must try to pass through that hallway of bitterness and come to face the facts. The next phase is when you have forgiven but haven't reconciled. This is the time when you are just waiting for that last push, a sign from the universe or a lifejacket to make you get through the passage and summon the strength to get back with your partner. Deep inside you, you have forgiven them and are either reluctant to take them back or you are waiting for them to repent more and then you take them back. The last situation you can find yourself in is when you neither reconcile nor forgive. This is sadly the end of the relationship. You or your spouse may run to the lawyers and file for divorce. No matter what situation you are in, learning to place your happiness above everything else is the most important. Understand this to be a wake-up call to start paying more attention and care to yourself.

Chapter 10: Examples for setting up a shooting path

Here are a few examples of situations that people have faced in their lives and what they can do to heal or react after finding out.

"He cheated on me and was unable to take responsibility for his actions or even admit it for that matter until I kept questioning him. I found out he cheated with two other women and he made the same excuses and now he is trying to get back together with me and is claiming he is a different person."

It is mostly construed that the betrayed is the only one in pain and needs to be healed. However, the offender may also shut down due to the guilt of cheating, and to cope with this they may end up blaming the other person. The narcissistic behavior may be caused due to certain events in their past or just their nature of fearing commitment. This has nothing to do with the betrayed. In addition, the betrayed must try to be aware of their emotions and feelings. The rage and the grief of losing someone they cared so much about should be patiently understood and dealt with. If this person returns after causing all the trauma, check if they are remorseful and don't rush into anything. Take it slow and maintain a continuous stream of conversations and discuss or point out any oddities you face in each other's behavior.

"I've been cheated on, lied to and abused by my ex-fiancé. I was 7 months pregnant with our daughter. One month after I gave birth I learned about his affair. He kept on denying it until he admitted the affair when he went back to his work on a cruise ship. It really hurts because we've been in a committed relationship for eleven years. He blamed everything on me. And he even dared to deny that he is the father. I told him no one had ever touched me except him and I'm willing to have my daughter undergo a DNA test to prove to him that he's the father. He kept accusing me of cheating on him when in fact he's the one who cheated."

This is extremely excruciating. Having a child while facing this situation makes it extremely hard to cope with. The first thing that needs to be done is to get help or get in touch with your family or some trusted person. The recent abandonment and indifference of the partner can be too much to handle. An expecting woman is already at a sensitive time in her life. So, the priority must be to lose correspondence with this cheating partner and find a safe environment where you are nurtured and loved. Having a child assures companionship between you and your child for life. This is precious. Even if the other person has the thought of shrugging off all responsibilities, you are enough. Visit a psychiatrist and have good and long therapeutic sessions to release inner emotions. Finances can be a big factor especially when an infant is involved. Sort your life out with the help of your loved ones and try to put your focus away from anything that reminds you of the unfaithful partner.

"When the mask slipped on my covert ex-wife and she left me and the children, I had no clue as to why. She was drinking and staying away from home and I thought that alcohol was the issue. As a consequence of my divorce, I discovered that my mother was covertly narcissistic and my ex-wife was one as well. My ex-wife never gave me any concrete reason why she left other than I "didn't change." What was I supposed to change into? A butterfly? It made no sense."

Women want emotional support, fairness, friendship and sensitivity in their relationship. Even though this seems a lot, but when you are entering into a relationship with a person, it is necessary to know and understand the person. A woman wants a man to have a good heart and work hard in the relationship. It may even be about having money or being attractive. She wants someone who loves her unconditionally who she can love back. However, it is necessary to look for signs if a person is dissatisfied with you. Any relationship, no matter how compatible, will suffer issues if couples don't talk about their feelings and emotions openly to each other. Ignoring one another while in the relationship only increases the distance between the partners. It is hard but the key is to actually understand what the other person expects of you, and to make a decision based on the possibility of fulfilling their expectations. Otherwise, it is a waste of time for both people.

"My boyfriend of three years told me he had been cheating on me for the last few months with some girl both physically and emotionally. He said he wasn't happy with me and that's why he did it. I did everything in the world to make this man happy. I was there for him through so much, including the passing of his mother. Most of our arguments centered on him always going out with friends, clubbing, drinking, and not spending enough time with me and making me feel special. He pointed out how "annoying and needy" I was when I asked for more in the relationship, which in turn caused him to be unhappy and seek out this other woman. I had this gut feeling all along and he told me I was crazy and couldn't be more wrong, and he repeatedly denied there was anything going on with them. Now I can't help but wonder how he gave everything we shared away to some other girl so easily."

Finding the person who you cared about so much and whose life you invested in turn away from you is unbearable. It can crush the nervous system of any person, and it's very common to feel belittled and dumb. The gush of emotions engulfing you can get the best of you. For the victim who is hurt, it is necessary to think about the moments in the relationship when the other person reciprocated their emotions. More likely than not, if the victim reflects, they may find out that the other person never showed the same level of affection and care as they did. The imbalance can make a person take you for granted and may construe you to be something of a pushover. This usually surfaces only after the shock of betrayal. The person who has gone out of the relationship starts to fear commitment because their partner is too present for them. This is completely the offender's fault, who is not clearly viewing the person in the same light as they are. Their real fault is that they could have ended the relationship by being transparent rather than cheating and then summoning the audacity to reveal their affair and blame the other person. The victim should have looked for signs of cheating earlier, and if nothing seemed suspicious, then such person is an obsessive cheater; no matter how attached they are, they are most likely to cheat repeatedly. The victim needs to accept the fact they should finally move on and refrain from letting self-doubt to clog their minds.

"Years ago, I was deeply in love with a guy and I thought that we would get married. When he left me, I honestly thought that I would die. I even considered suicide. It took me three years to get over him. I am now married to a wonderful man and I am happy. I rarely think about my ex these days, and I know that I have forgiven him because I don't hate him anymore. I hope that he has found as much happiness as I have. It's a cliché, but it is so true that time is a healer."

Time truly heals. It's about attaining maturity and controlling your emotions from getting the best of you in the situation. Once your partner cheats, the adrenaline rush that flows through the body makes you either shut down or become violently aggressive. You can get drawn into these emotions and may get as down as wishing to end your life. But what is important is at those moments you just hold on to something positive in you. It shouldn't be external, it has to be internal. A strong mind and a drive to live a better life independently must motivate you to reach a better phase in your life. Take this as an experience where you learn something and not let it paralyze or scar you for good. This is not the only relationship that you will have in your life. You need to work towards getting your confidence back and know your worth. No one should be so important that they claim a right over your life. Everyone is sufficient for themselves. The feeling of ending up alone is an irrational fear that the mind creates, and the other person becomes irreplaceable. However, they can be replaced by someone capable of loving you even more than them and you can have the life you deserve with them.

"Getting cheated on by the person who talks about how much they love you is the worst thing ever. Although I've been cheated on once by the person I adore, I found it in my heart to give him another chance, and as time passes by, we've been doing way much better. Communication and understanding and love are much stronger."

Marriage is not easy. Even if it is a happy one, there is no manual on how to navigate through all the challenges that will come your way. Couples have to learn each other's needs and basic nature, and most importantly, communicate well. Communicating may sometimes be too hard to do, but the better the communication, the lesser is the build-up and the less fights. It is a personal choice to take back a person who cheated on you. It must be a well-rounded decision and must be done for all the right reasons. To stay together amidst societal pressures is not a good idea. This can hamper everyone who surrounds them - their family members, friends or children. If a couple is still emotionally dependent, they should be willing and ready to work on their differences. Transparency is promised and kept, and communication about any issues faced by either are welcomed and discussed properly.

"I can only talk for myself, it took three years to forgive and five years to regain trust. Even then it can only be achieved if the person that cheated shows genuine remorse, which in my case was very strong."

It is wrong to think that the relationship is surely over after one cheats on another. Betrayal can be one of the most difficult things to get over in a relationship. A third person who enters the relationship is now forming a part of the dynamic, and it is difficult to get past that feeling of your loved one allowing someone else to enter your marriage. However, it is possible to make amends. The support system has to be rebuilt. Trust needs to be regained, and the unfaithful must ensure that they will never go outside the relationship again. It is very difficult to form trust and surpass the pain. However, with full disclosure and by providing a safer environment for the other person, this can be achieved.

Chapter 11: I still believe in our relationship

You don't want to let go. You still have faith in the relationship. You wish to get your partner to forgive you and get rid of the resentment they have towards you, and you want to give your marriage a chance. This becomes difficult. The spouse can't seem to forgive you and can't get over the hurt they are feeling. The first step in rebuilding the relationship is to get over this hurt and resentment. It can be caused by your affair or humiliating them in public in some way, or due to some specific behavior that you displayed to them. The resentment towards you has something to do with what you have done to them in the past, and as a reaction to which they are still treating you in a disrespectful way. You may not have cared about their feelings. It can even be mental or physical abuse or lack of intimacy. People gets focused on stressful points in their lives and tend to neglect their spouse.

They have a tendency to shut down in front of you. They stop responding to you emotionally. There can be a lack of communication. One of the prime reasons that's causing these negative feelings to grow is lack of intimacy. This includes sex and also simple affection. Perhaps your partner doesn't want to touch or doesn't want to be touched or hugged or kissed. Sometimes spouses tell them that they are physically repulsed by them. This is the ultimate sign of hurt and lack of forgiveness. They may start to put other things ahead of you in the relationship. They feel other things are of a higher priority. It can be their children, other family members or friends, or even their hobbies, their business or their career. Ideally, the relationship must be one of the highest-ranking priorities in both people's lives. They may intentionally hurt you, and it may seem impossible for you to make them forgive you. They may be alienating you from your children or close friends or family members. Many may start to overspend. This is called financial sabotage. They intend to cause hurt to the other person after the other person hurt them. So, this creates a barrier between the two of you. It makes communication, trust and intimacy almost impossible. Therefore, you need to eliminate these barriers in order to move forward.

Another thing that may be triggered is that it causes you to behave in the same way. You may also start holding back and emotionally shut down. Check your partner's behavior and begin to analyze the pattern of resentment that they are displaying. This can give you clues on how to deal with it. First is when your partner wants to forgive you but doesn't know how. They recognize they are hurting, and they can't forgive you. They know their behavior isn't helping you, but genuinely don't know what to do about it. The way to know this is to ask yourself, is your partner aware that they can't forgive you? Does the inability to forgive make them feel bad? Does it appear that they seriously want to do something about it and they want to get over the hurt and resentment towards you, and they are assuming some responsibility in trying to do this? The other type of resentment which is fairly common is when they don't want to forgive you. Even if they say they want to. They are in such a position that they use their apparent pain to punish the other person. They are saying you hurt me; I won't forgive you until you receive some punishment. So, they will punish you by staying hurt because they know that hurts you too. This is a very prevalent belief that people have. It is a way of maintaining control over you and the relationship. They are meaning to tell you how you feel, and this can take a destructive turn. You need to ask yourself, are they in a place where they can ever actually forgive you? You will be able to answer this easily based on their behavior and feelings and actions.

    True forgiveness is removing all the pain and traces of the pain from the outer world and the inner world as well. To forgive, you need to completely get rid of all the remains of the pain surrounding what caused the hurt. It has to be unconditional. They have to say it doesn't matter what happens, they are going to let go and come back to you. It is acknowledging what happened and then sticking together and not letting the emotions of abandoning the person overpower you. This is the ultimate goal. It is achievable. Let's begin by stating that you must be sorry for what you did wrong, or whoever did wrong must have repented in their heart. That behavior needs to stop. If you had an affair, you need to stop everything you had with that person. You can't realistically expect to not be apologetic and your partner to forgive you. If the husband goes and cheats and the wife forgives, after half a dozen times, she stops forgiving and he wonders, why is she no longer forgiving me and is cynical. There has to be genuine remorse and a genuine want to not hurt the person anymore. If you do have a pattern of repeating what causes your partner to get hurt, you need to identify the cause that's stirring you to do it. You need to repair that element. It's not about dealing with forgiveness, it's about dealing with the pattern.

Certain myths need to be busted when dealing with the grey area of forgiveness in cases of infidelity. To think that time will heal and the relationship will restore to its former glory—this is true to some extent. This can often be used as an excuse by a person to not do much. The person just wallows in self-pity. However, like any change, healing from hurt can be done quickly. The betrayed would need to have deeply and truly forgiven the other person. To do that, there has to be the right environment and the right mindset, and healing can come fairly quickly. You need to give it as much time as it needs. The process can be sped up depending on what you do and how you do it. Another myth is that it is up to the betrayed person to deal with. It's their problem, and you leave them and let yourself have time to soak it in and decide what you want to do. Having the unfaithful person take responsibility is certainly important. The problem is that if it's left to the victim alone to deal with, they might not know what to do and the timing is going to be based on their time frame. You are not giving them any support. It should be explained that it is up to them to deal with the situation, but you are there to help and support them every step of the way. You are waiting for them to come back. But this shouldn't be misconstrued as you apologizing all the time and crowding them. This will have a repellent effect. So, you need to find a balance to deal with the situation effectively. You are giving all of your power to them. What they need to get over the pain and hurt is some strength. You are making yourself weak, which is in turn, making the whole situation weak. There is nothing to pull them up here.

    What can you do to try to get them to forgive you? Make sure to not take responsibility for their feelings. Your spouse needs to take responsibility for their feelings. They may not want to or may say that they can't. But true healing and forgiveness can never happen if it is not coming to them internally. The way to do this is telling them that you are sorry, and you are ready to take responsibility. You will make sure it doesn't happen again, but ultimately, it's up to you to be completely transparent. You can say you love them, and you want to help but you can't force them to forgive you. They need to take responsibility for that. Next is to forgive yourself.

You may have baggage on your shoulders and the guilt is eating you up inside and you may lose face and sleep. You did make a mistake. You are human. Everyone makes mistakes. This is not to negate the mistake in any sense. Accept and forgive yourself for that. You have assured them and yourself that it is never going to happen again. Make sure you are doing your best that it never happens again. Don't feel guilty. Guilt never does any good for anyone. Next, you need to acknowledge and resolve. Acknowledge to your partner that you did them wrong and tell them that is completely your wish to heal the relationship. It will be made better and will get back to what it was. Do this powerfully and firmly so that they know you mean business. At this point, it won't be advisable to ask them how they feel. They have done that over and over and revealed to you how sick they are feeling. Tell them how you feel. You are hopeful and willing to make amends. You resolve that things will change for the better and they will be better. The next step is to ask them to acknowledge that you are both human and you both are capable of making mistakes. Do this in a general and non-confrontational way. Tell them that you have acknowledged what you have done, and you resolve that you want things to get better. You have made mistakes, but they make mistakes too. You are not accusing them, but you are reminding them in a non-confrontational way. What you are doing is that you are getting them to acknowledge another side of what happened. There are always two sides to everything between a couple. The effect of what you are doing here will ideally diffuse some of the resentment and rationalize their fears a little bit. They might begin to see it's not fully your fault. You made a mistake and it's not the end of the world.

The last step lies in creating a positive healing environment. When we have a lot of problems in a relationship, that's what we are focused on. It just creates an endless cycle of problems, hurt, pain and misery. Now that you have acknowledged it's their responsibility to work on healing, and resolved to forgive yourself, this step is about moving on. You don't need to focus on this stuff anymore. Focus on creating a positive environment. Refuse to focus on the negative. Whatever you wish to achieve, that's what you get. If you want to heal things, just focus on the positives. The correct way to do so is if they seem upset, don't apologize. You give them support but don't continue to say sorry to them. Just move the focus away from that. Another way is to be attractive. Show your mental strength. If you are happy and optimistic, you are not being cynical. You have acknowledged you made a mistake. Now you can be happy and optimistic about the future.

Don't dwell on the problems. It is necessary to be loving towards your partner, but not in a weak way. You need to restore your pre-affair state of affairs. Don't react to negativity. Tell them that you love them, but you are not going to react to the negativity. That's the greatest gift you can give to anybody—that they are responsible for their own feelings. You worry about how you feel and let them worry about how they feel.

The harsh reality is that about 44% of married men and 34% of married women have had affairs in their lives. The younger you are, the more likely you are to have an affair. It can happen at any stage, however. Is honesty a far-fetched concept? How important is honesty in any relationship? It's obvious. It is something that we learned since our childhood: honesty is the best policy. It has an even deeper and more powerful meaning in a relationship. In a relationship, it means two people living as their true and authentic selves without fear of the consequences. It involves the other person to do the same unconditionally. First and foremost, are you living an authentic life? Are you being who you are? Take an example of someone you admire. What distinguishes them from the rest of us? I think one of the reasons why we get attracted to such people is that they are living their true life irrespective of any criticism or negativity from others. They are being themselves and they are happy to be themselves.

Something that tends to hold us back in our relationship is fear. The fear of what we might feel can happen, fear of being criticized, or being hurt or making mistakes. We have to get to a place where there is no fear of real honesty to start happening. See if this allows the other person to do the same unconditionally. It means not just being yourself but allowing the other person to be themselves too. Allow them to make their own mistakes so that they know what is true to them without being offended or hurt by it. Can you imagine being in the relationship and being able to say anything you wanted and not intentionally wanting to hurt the other person? If you can and you feel you will never be judged by them for that, and you can live your life developing yourself, imagine the huge positive impact that is going to have on yourself and everyone else around you. If you are facing the fear that your partner is not being completely honest with you, the place to start in that situation is with yourself. You need to ask yourself honest questions. Why do you think they are not being honest with you? Are they able to express the feelings to you without the fear of consequences? Are you living your true self without any fear?

Maybe in a relationship, you are still unaware of the depth of honesty that you can achieve. This can make a big difference in the quality of your relationship. Ask yourself these questions: Are you able to share every thought you ever had with them? Are there any thoughts that you haven't been able to share with them? However big or small. If your spouse asks you what you are doing or thinking, are you always totally honest with them? Have you ever not said something to your spouse, but you are thinking about it? Have you had a sexual fantasy more than once and will you be able to tell your spouse about it? Can you explain it to them in great detail without getting embarrassed? (And without finding this too daunting). There are very few honest marriages. Don't feel bad if you aren't there, because you are not alone. The first step is to identify your standing and the extent of honesty you both share. If you are not living in a relationship based on total honesty, you will feel caged. You can't be completely happy because you are bottling up your feelings and not letting them out. There are consequences for your spouse when you are not completely honest with them. They are going to be frustrated and confused. There will be miscommunication between you two due to the reluctance in speaking from your heart out to each other. The whole thing of shared growth is going to be lacking from the relationship. You need to have the liberty to make mistakes and learn from them. If you are unable to do that, you are going to reach a saturation point and the relationship won't be able to sustain itself. It's so worth trying to achieve an open honest relationship. You will be able to make yourself happy. You won't have to worry before trying new things. You and your spouse can take risks together. You can discover each other and have the best experiences in life that you could wish for.

Chapter 12: Ten Steps to Happiness

1) Decide if it is worth forgiving. This step is the most important. Before recovering from the incident, you need to understand if it is important. No matter how much you love him/her, to forgive a betrayal is the most difficult challenge you can face. Here are some possible reasons to forgive. It happened only once. Maybe you fought, and he/she, after drinking a glass too many, ended up in bed with another person. Your partner is sorry for what happened, is depressed and would do anything to prove their repentance. If you think you have a really special relationship, it's better to resist the temptation to leave to see if you can recover it. You don't want to give up your relationship, especially if you've been with this person for a long time and your relationship is healthy and intimate. Discovering a betrayal, of course, will put all this in doubt, but you should analyze the

whole story before making a decision.

Don't ever forgive a serial traitor. If they have already done it and you have children and a life together, it's not worth it. Maybe it's the first time you have caught them, but they have betrayed you many times already. Additionally, do not forgive a betrayal if you are in a new relationship with someone. It will be almost impossible to build a solid relationship on this foundation. If betrayal is a sign of a relationship destined to fail, do not try hard. Two people who have nothing in common, who do not feel very attracted to each other and who are unable to make the relationship work, have no future. You may get reminded of the betrayal at certain moments, which may make you leave them and never see them again. In those times, focus on what is tying you to the person. Recognize their remorse and urge them to make amends as part of your healing process, and also reflect on your inner self. It is necessary that it's not just a compromise and that you feel happy. It is pointless to still be in the relationship and make the other person feel sorry all the time or expect them to be apologetic every step of the way.

2) Take the time to calm down after the initial chaos. You don't want to talk about it right away or argue about it. That could make things worse for you as well the unfaithful spouse. Take a walk, go to the gym or cry in your room. Distract yourself as much as possible. You may want to express your anger or do something that harms the person. On the contrary, you may even get inclined towards causing harm upon yourself. Be aligned with these emotions, and then think rationally, so that you don't act upon these raw emotions. This process could take a few weeks, so you should move away from them. If you live together, stay at the home of a friend or family member or in a hotel. Take some time off and lose any kind of contact with them. Be ready to face them only after taking some time off to come to terms with the situation. You can be filled with doubts and questions at this point, so creating a distraction rather than overthinking is preferred. Thinking about why

this happened with you both, and how you could have overlooked this happening all this time, can cloud your brain. You may feel a pressing need to talk to the person, but it is much better to refrain from this to find some peace. Don't blame yourself.

3) Don't think your partner has betrayed you because you're not attractive or interesting, or because of work, or that you let your children absorb your energy too much. The fault of the betrayal is of the person who betrays. However, although it is not your fault, you may have done something to contribute to the degradation of the relationship. Every human being is allowed to make mistakes. But no excuse can be big enough to involve someone other than your partner in your life. The cheating partner can manipulate you by shifting the light on your mistakes. If a couple faces any problems and they can't deal with them appropriately, they should leave each other. There is always an option to leave your partner because you both aren't happy. If you are the single person who is

unhappy with your partner, own up to your decision to leave them. Then search for someone else or pursue another dear relationship in your life. If they provide an excuse for your shortcomings then that can be argued by saying if that were the case, the concerns should have been discussed openly. If the discussion doesn't go well or the other person still refuses to change, they can end the relationship and move on. Never let the traitor blame you. If that happens, cut the thread off without thinking twice. If you cheated on your partner first and you still stay together only to find out your partner is cheating on you, it's unfair. This is not acceptable and ideally you must move away from this person. If you as a couple couldn't get past the initial cheating, you should have not come together and tried to make it work. It is not exemplary to take revenge on the person by cheating on them to make them taste their own medicine.

4) Finance and financial pressures can ruin a relationship. There may be a change in

circumstances such as you losing a job, you find out your assets are undervalued, their expenses are a lot higher than what they used to be. If people have incurred additional costs as a couple, they may have gotten involved in things that are costing them more money. These can create financial problems. Another problem can be that we have higher expectations and increasing needs. There is nothing wrong with wanting more, but debt can be very easy to come by through big credit card bills or other expenses. They may start mounting up, and before we know it, the pressure becomes too much. Ironically, people increase their expenditure at times of being under pressure, which really gets them stuck in a vicious cycle. If you are not feeling good and you are looking for ways to alleviate the pressure, you might book a trip or go out for a movie or restaurant, which can make you spend more money and worsen your situation.

When you first enter a relationship, you don't have any financial burdens, but the pressure starts to build up eventually. What has changed? You have goals and things you want to achieve together. If you want to make a commitment to staying together, you want to build a life together. A big part of our lives is finance management. You want to buy a house or have a place to raise your children and develop a lifestyle. As more of these things come along, they all add to financial cost. Things tend to cost more than we expect them to. Things are going to invariably cost more, because if you are buying a house, you will also have to buy things to fill up the empty spaces. Raising children is very expensive. Specifically, men and women behave differently when facing financial pressures. Women facing this burden would like to talk it out. They express their feelings in words. If you are a man and a woman is describing her financial problems, the man needs to know that she is not looking for a solution necessarily. They tend to process their thoughts out loud. That's a completely opposite reaction to that of men. Men usually shut down when they are under financial pressures. Men have this attitude that it is their personal responsibility to solve all the problems in the marriage. They are biologically wired to achieve goals of a perfectly stable lifestyle. Go back to caveman days when the man's role was to go out and hunt for food. So, having financial problems can pose a problem to their masculinity because it hasn't been solved and it hits their self-esteem. This is an obvious generalization and may not hold true in every case in exactitude. But you can see some patterns of this behavior in your marriage. You should understand that they are just trying to deal with the problem as individuals and it has nothing to do with you. If you find out that financial pressures are affecting your marriage, be more aware of how you are addressing this issue. You may view your financial burden as something that you can individually deal with and not let that affect your marriage. You assume that you shouldn't bring your problems back home or you must share everything with your spouse, maintaining the sanctity of marriage, and think it will be ideal. Instead, acknowledge the problem. Don't brush it aside or pretend it doesn't exist. Don't try to suppress your awareness or focus.

You need to start becoming financially educated. Start from setting financial goals. You can sit down with your spouse and plan out what you want to achieve. Check how much you have and pay off any debts first. Set a date for when you want to pay off or collect a certain amount of savings. The next step is to reduce your expenses and increase your savings. See what you can cut out and what you don't particularly value. In this process, you will realize that you have started valuing money. Then you can aspire to increase your income. It can be achieved in so many ways today. You don't have to worry about getting a raise or picking up more jobs. You can sell things on eBay and do a number of things online. You can easily find some fun new ways of increasing your income. The next step is to agree with your partner to share your goals, and you both take responsibility to achieve the ultimate result. It's important for both the parties to not blame and actually engage in providing for each other's needs. They can also resolve so much by providing each other with support. If you are a woman, you can get more involved (if you aren't already) and take initiative to inculcate financial values. You can give your husband an idea and input. Men must agree to share the responsibility so that this doesn't become the reason for the end of your relationship.

5) Make sure your partner is willing to recover the relationship. If you decide to forgive him, you will need to make sure that he wants to resume the journey with you, even if it takes months or years to start feeling good again. Make sure your partner is genuinely sorry. There is a beautiful difference between saying and being sorry. Make sure that, in addition to being sorry, he is willing to stay with you. A real sense of happiness can be achieved if you stop getting intimidated by the fear of the relationship ending or getting a divorce. If the

thought of splitting up makes you anxious, angry or depressed, then you probably have certain fears about it. This is not a judgment because fears are completely natural. But these fears can't help you. Common fears while people are trying to get a divorce are security or emotional fears. Security fears include if you get divorced, where will you live? How will I earn money, raise children, make a good lifestyle? How will children deal with divorce? Men may worry about their finances splitting and clever lawyers hired by their wives. Comprehend which of these fears applies to you. Emotional fears can be about how you will feel if you get a divorce. Some of these fears are what will society think of me—friends, colleagues, family? Will you be able to keep your friends? What if they outcast you and feel like they don't want anything to do with you again? Will your children still love you? Will you be able to provide the same upbringing which your spouse and you could have provided together? Are they going to turn out well-adjusted? Will you ever find love again? Is it too painful to get a divorce? These are the questions to ask if you have any of these thoughts applying to your life.

However, if you really want to save your marriage, you need to stop worrying about it coming to an end. Because the fear will keep your mind off the process of actually making that change. It's said that whatever you fear will come upon you. Fear makes you weak and when you are weak you are unattractive. Your spouse will be likely to leave you. Fear makes you reactive and not proactive. If you just react and you fall in the downward spiral of things, it will be very difficult to recover your marriage. This can drive you to do all the wrong things rather than the right things. It can stop you from dealing with the reality of your situation. You can either recover or get back your lost love, or else your relationship will probably come to an end. One of these things is going to happen; it will either be sooner or later. People tend to get complacent that everything will be fine along the way. But this situation never lasts forever.

Because eventually one person will get sick of how things are or some better alternative comes along in their lives. You need to be prepared for both these situations. It is best to prepare for any situation that may come your way. Having overcome your fear will help you rise to the occasion much better. To get rid of your fears, look at each of your fears clearly and see which of these are actually true. We sometimes imagine that something is going to happen, but it isn't the case. Ask yourself: don't you have your close ones who love you enough to be there for you at this time of atrocity? Create a positive picture without any negativity from the spouse. Just include the positive points. This is not to encourage yourself to either get divorced or stay together necessarily, but it will make you positive and bring you to a much more attractive place in your life. You will feel rejuvenated rather than sulking and feeling vulnerable.

6) You will both have to acknowledge your feelings and accept the pain and confusion that you will not miss. Tell them how you feel and

make sure they know what is happening to you. Before you can recover the relationship, your partner will have to understand that they have put you in a terrible position. Of course, even they are not in a good place, but make sure they understand you. Some people have real issues in their marriage. They have fallen out of love and the communication is gone, and the sexual attraction is not there anymore. Of course, the biggest challenge is the affair itself. The most difficult situation is when one person really tries to save the marriage and the other really doesn't want to stay. When a person is still holding on to the relationship and really trying to repair it to make the spouse happy, they feel all the problems will come to an end. Even though this is true, many people focus on pleasing their spouse without comforting themselves. They are putting their own needs last, and this is especially true in the case of women. They put their children and husband before them, but in the process they themselves become miserable. This does more harm than good. If you place another's needs before your own, you will end up unhappy, which will increase your stress. You will feel depressed, and your heath, productivity and work will suffer. It can also strain your other relationships. You may eventually begin to be resentful towards your spouse. You have been putting all this effort in, and either you fail to get anything back or you simply are not getting the result you want. Being sad and unhappy makes you look unattractive to the other person. This will make you both unhappy and the relationship won't be able to sustain itself. The important thing to save here is your soul. Here soul is not being used in a religious sense at all. You have to keep intact and really save the essence of who you are. What does it look like to be really who you are? It begins with doing things that you really love to do. You spend your life and time in things that you enjoy doing. You are able to speak your mind and say out loud everything you want without having the fear of being criticized. You are confident and you realize everyone's reaction to what you say or feel is really their own concern. You must do the things that make you happy. Learning to be and enjoy is the most important thing to do.

7) Talk about what happened honestly. Don't rush into the conversation. It is not about arguing, but about discussing it rationally: Ask him what happened. He does not need to go into intimate details but must tell you how many times he has seen the other person and when. Ask him what he feels about the other person. Your partner might tell you that he doesn't want to share anything, but then you'll have to make sure of it. Ask him if it happened before you found out, so you'll know more before making a final decision. Knowing the past doesn't always help, but the damage is done now. Ask him what he thinks of your relationship. Find out why he cheated and what his intentions are. Repeat how you feel. At this point, you have already communicated your emotions widely, but maybe you have changed your mind after hearing the whole story. Discuss what to do to

make the relationship work. You could take notes and figure out what mistakes to avoid for you to get stronger. Spend more time together, be honest or completely change your routine. You can go to a psychologist, talk about your problems with your friends or work out everything yourself. Set rules. If your partner cheated on you at work, do they have to change jobs? Many experts say yes. Does your partner have to call you often when he is out? This could be humiliating, but remember that you have also received your dose of humiliation.

8) Work on having more open communication every day: Talk about your true feelings at least once a week. This step should not be forced, but do not underestimate it. Tell yourself how you feel. Talk about both positive and negative emotions, even if you have distanced yourself after the betrayal. Don't be passive-aggressive. If you are angry, say it when it's time. The problem people have when they start to see their marriage fail is they simply don't know what to do. You are currently faced

with the prospect of ending your relationship for some reason. Probably the two of you have just drifted apart. It has taken time and you are not connecting the same way as you used to. There is no fulfillment or enjoyment left in the marriage. Have you tried counseling or therapy for your relationship? Are you discussing your problems with your spouse or trying to discuss them? Have you pleaded with them or threatened them? Have you done any nice things for them? Have you tried to make them feel guilty? Then see if any of these actually worked. Have they had a positive impact? Has this brought you closer together or has it gone the opposite way and made things worse? If all these things don't work, then what does work? Understanding the answer to that comes down to one thing—you have to let go of the need to save your marriage. You need to focus on yourself and really care about your present and future.

9) Work on improving the relationship. You will have to cultivate the relationship. Here's

what to try: Devote yourself to an interest or a hobby together. Share more interests. If you have distanced yourself because you have nothing in common, choose something to bring you closer, like choosing a book each month that you will read or watch a TV show together. It seems little, but you will notice the difference. Make compromises. In a relationship, both should win. Go on vacation together. Doing something new will be a breath of fresh air. A journey is not a long-term solution, but it will give you time to reflect and to be alone together. Stop blaming your partner. It may seem impossible, but if you want things to work between you, you won't have to blame their mistakes. Talk about it only when you tell them how you feel. Don't humiliate your partner or push them to make sure they understand your love over and over again: this is exhausting.

10) Do not be obsessed with the person with whom your partner has betrayed you, or you will go crazy and ruin the relationship. If you know them and you go to the same social outings,

avoid meeting them. Strive to forget their existence. Don't compare yourself to this person and feel inferior to their alleged qualities. Don't judge them if you don't know them. Maybe they fell in love with your partner or didn't know they were married. Don't follow them on Facebook or on other social networks trying to understand what they have that you don't have. Don't even follow them in real life. Don't talk about them with your partner. Focus on your relationship. If you are obsessed with this person and you can't help it, talk to a friend. Stop.

Chapter 13: Conclusions

When two people meet in a relationship with an element of passion that sustains them and their union ends in marriage, they may not be aware of what is to follow. Sometimes they may have difficulty keeping everything together or reconciling. Love is messy and infidelity is even more disorderly. To ensure normality again, it is necessary to have something to hold onto. Some infidelities resolve quickly, but some may have difficulty ending. This reluctance must be worked out. People who want to rebuild the relationship after the unfaithfulness are on a hard journey. At the time of being destroyed, you don't trust what the unfaithful says. You lose confidence in others and in yourself. It is a loss of a partner and a loss of self. Try to find a purpose and never lose hope. If the person left you without giving you the answers you deserved, embrace it. Feel hurt and move on. A healthy and safe future awaits you.

Having a relationship without criticism, without resentment, without cheating is just a place where you two will be happy to be together and support each other. Each of us should try to reach that place in our relationships where there is complete honesty and space to breathe. If you feel that being honest is difficult or unworkable for you, there are a few things you can do to significantly increase the amount of honesty and enjoy all the good things in your relationship. The first is to be honest with yourself and to yourself. The relationship you have with others is a reflection of yours with yourself. If you want something in life and you think you can't tell your spouse, maybe because they may not approve, then move that thought away; just ask yourself what you really want here. Imagine it theoretically, and it becomes really clear. So, imagine the worst thing that can happen if you tell your partner what you're hiding. You may think they will get angry. Maybe they will or not. But if they get angry, they will have to deal with it and the chances are they will get over it.

Getting angry is something that can be addressed. So, you have to understand what the best thing is that could happen. You can actually get what you want and share happiness with your partner. An example of this is when a husband in therapy revealed that he wanted to go to a nudist beach and go scuba diving and sunbathing. He felt embarrassed to say it out loud because he feared his wife would judge him. So, it is really necessary to provide total honesty. The next step is to create an environment of trust. You decide to never make your spouse feel bad about what they say or do. Don't judge them for their thoughts and feelings. Allow them to make mistakes. The last step is to guarantee total honesty from this point onwards.

I wish you the best of luck, and I hope this has helped your soul to heal and your relationship to become stronger.

Thank you for purchasing this book, and I hope that reading it was an interesting and educational experience. I put all my efforts, enthusiasm and heart into every sentence I wrote. The main objective of this book is to help, with my experience, my readers to understand and overcome betrayal, which is a profound and devastating malaise. If you liked it, and above all, it influenced your life and helped you along the way, I ask you for five minutes of your time to write down what you think of the book by leaving a review, because it would help other people improve their lives. The opinions of my readers are ones I always treasure for my work, and it would help me improve my way of communicating and give me new ideas to develop.

CODEPENDENCY NO MORE

How to cure codependency, stop controlling others and caring for Yourself

Part 1

Chapter 1: Anatomy of Codependent Relationships

The term 'Codependency' can be traced back to the 1980s and there are so many different meanings and definitions for the disorder. Codependency is an individualistic disorder that is expressed in relationships. Codependency doesn't manifest unless you are connected to another person. It is not a personality type.

If you find yourself using these derogatory phrases, such as "she is needy," or "he is pathetic," and you connect it to codependency, that could not be further from the truth. There are many types of codependents, and codependency comes in multiple shapes and forms. Codependents can be simply defined as people who are hyper-focused on giving love, respect, and care freely and abundantly to others while undervaluing, dismissing, or not demanding the same from other people.

They want an equal distribution of respect, love, and care in their relationships, but they don't know how to get it. The desire for equality ties them to the relationship. They are often with a person who is unable to reciprocate their feelings. They resent that person, but still maintain the relationship. There can be active codependents who pursue another person who tries to control them, but both styles of codependency share the same psychological and relational traits. They stay in a relationship, giving freely and abundantly to others while not receiving the same level of care from their partner.

The term codependency has been overused and has often become harmful in the way people use it. It has morphed into a stereotype. Codependents are individuals who have problems; they feel stuck, hurt, and ignored. It is very important to recognize that they have a disorder. They are struggling to find care, love, and respect but can't find it, and sometimes don't recognize it when they do. People use codependent as a pejorative and negative term. It often carries a stigma.

Most codependent people are people pleasers. They are really empathetic and are doers in a real sense. They are the people who want to fix others; they don't even think twice before doing something they are asked of. They tend to do way more than they should. They struggle to find the balance between helping someone and taking care of themselves.

Even though it is great to give to other people and help them, it is coming from an unhealthy place of feeling empty and giving for the wrong reasons—it is not the same as being genuinely altruistic. When you are giving and you end up feeling resentful or absolutely exhausted, this is a signal that you are not doing it for the right reasons. When you are not in tune with yourself, you can't satisfy others. A good place to give is from a place of self-satisfaction, which can also be perceived as a genuine need to help someone. When you give because you have always just given and don't know how to refuse to help someone, those are indicators of codependency.

One aspect of this behavior is a constant need for validation. While growing up, a child needs validation. It can come from their parents or their guardians. They need validation about what they think and that how they feel is okay. As a little kid who feels something, it's important that even when parents don't agree with him, he is still validated when it comes to his feelings. If you don't want to give him an extra piece of chocolate to eat and he gets angry, it is important that you make him feel that his reaction is perfectly normal.

Your will should not be imposed on him in order to satisfy the dominance of your thoughts. This will severely hamper the development of your child. The majority of codependents never received this validation growing up, or didn't get it consistently. This is why they seek it outside of themselves, and most of these people develop codependency. You can carry co-dependence tendencies. 'Is what I am doing okay? How does this look?' These questions are something that you are seeking outside of yourself.

A client once mentioned how she would clean her house constantly. Her husband would appreciate her for doing a great job, or for the food she made. While it is good to receive compliments from people, when those compliments become necessary for you to feel okay, that's not acceptable. You should know how to give them to yourself. It is healthy to get complimented, but if it didn't happen, could you do it yourself? How would you feel if you did it for yourself? Can you give yourself a pat on your back for cooking dinner that tastes so good? Upon hearing this, the client replied, "*It's nice to hear it from someone else.*"

This is true. It is really great to hear it from someone else. But we first have to learn how to do it for our own selves. It is necessary to have this sense of self-validation, so that when we receive this compliment from someone, it feels good, but not as an amazing fix to your own sense of self-worth. What should feel amazing is the validation you give to your own self. I got up early, went to the office, came back, cleaned, cooked dinner and ate. I am amazing. I can do this and more. That's a fantastic person right there. If you start applying this in your life, you will soon come to realize how seldom you are seeking that validation from others now.

Another characteristic of codependents is that they are fixers. They jump right in and start fixing a problem that is not even theirs. They overextend themselves without thinking about what's best for them. They take on other people's problems like they are their own. These people have a natural dash of empathy in their nature. When encountered with a problem, their initial response is to dive right in. This can be a major cause of resentment, because the person may not even want the problem to get fixed.

When you get involved where your opinion is not asked for, you aren't directly affected. Even if you do everything you can to solve it, the other person might not perceive this as genuine help. They may think of it as an unnecessary intrusion. This can cause you to feel hurt. It is not your job to jump in and take control over someone's life and actions, or mend something that is not your issue.

The codependent fixer is not uncommon. They work to fix other people's issues because they aren't happy if others aren't happy. Everyone needs to be okay for them to feel good. Therefore, if you are facing some problem, they need to make it right so that they, themselves, feel right. They won't feel good if you don't feel good. This is codependency at its core. They obviously don't want their friends or family to be unhappy, so they go straight to giving advice or offering help in whichever way possible. Their need to fix is very difficult to get rid of.

Codependents try to please people to get their validation. They struggle to say 'no' to anyone who asks them for help. The reason why they refrain from saying 'no' is that they don't want people to think poorly of them. They fear that if their turn comes up to ask someone else for a favor, that someone will turn away from them. It is unhealthy to continually give to others and not keep anything for yourself. We need to come from a place where we are motivating ourselves enough, before we can truly do that for others. When you do it for yourself, you don't need anyone else to do it for you. That is truly being healthy and whole by yourself.

People-pleasing is a by-product of insecurity. The thought becomes that if they refuse to do something for someone, they might end up losing that person's trust. Honestly, that person won't think any less of you. If someone stops loving you because you don't agree to do something for them, it is an indicator that maybe that person is unhealthy and shouldn't be in your life to begin with. So many clients guiltily speak about losing a close friend or broken relationship with a lot of shame because they couldn't be there for that person. But anyone who *really* loves you wouldn't place guilt on you for not doing something for them.

Chapter 2: You Are Not Insane—You Are Codependent

Every relationship in our lives affects us in one way or the other. Because we live in real-time and not in reflective times, where we reflect on every sphere of every relationship we look back on things *after* we get ahead of them. No, you are not crazy, you are just intoxicated by a narcissist's poisonous words. Whenever one gets in dialogue with a codependent, they may begin their sentence by saying things like, "This may sound stupid, or crazy, or unbelievable…"

Most people who have suffered at the hands of an emotional manipulator, whether it was their parent, boss, friend, family member, or a partner, may well have begun their sentences using these words, at one time or another. You are far from alone in how you feel. How you are feeling when you lead into your sentence in such a way is not stupid.

Unfortunately, being codependent is very real in our society, and emotional and psychological abuse is hard to see, let alone treat. Even if there is physical abuse present, the way narcissists shift blame or use reactive abuse against codependents can confuse the issue. It becomes very hard to discuss it with others outside of the relationship.

Sexual abuse is also very difficult to open up about. You are not now, nor were you ever crazy. You just loved, cared, trusted, and respected the toxic words of a manipulator. You did not possess enough knowledge to understand who they are, what they do, or the red flag warning signs. They have a personality disorder. If they are your parents, you are raised to believe this is normal. We end up accepting behavior as normal that we should have never tolerated.

Yet, most often adults who were raised by a narcissist will say that something just didn't feel right. How can a child know exactly what the feeling was, when they were being taught by the very person who made them feel this way? Similarly, having narcissistic partners who start by treating you very nicely and then slowly infect your mind and bring you down... your instincts may be speaking volumes, but you can't always comprehend what they are telling you.

There are conflicting events that happen to people in an emotionally abusive relationship. Emotional abuse is not physical, but a lot of physical abuse can also happen in such relationships. When you are being struck in the face, it might leave a mark and will hurt. Psychological abuse hurts us differently, in the most unimaginable ways, and we don't see it happening.

You can feel physical pain. Psychological abuse causes confusion and pain to occur in our minds and souls. Both types of abuse can leave a lot of side effects such as anxiety, trauma bonding, and post-traumatic stress disorder. The relationship starts with the narcissist wanting you all to themselves. While this may not always be the case, it is a common indicator. When they want you all to themselves, it is a major red flag.

The first stage of love bombing is when they can't seem to get enough of you. When they treat you so well, you can't get enough of them either. When you go out with your friends, it may start from them offering you a lift to keep an eye on you, and yet you believe they are just being kind. Then they might start to make you feel guilty for going, so you stop going out altogether. Further into the relationship, they may start with arguments, the silent treatment, or accusations.

Ultimately, you end up cutting yourself off from your friends and family due to the fear of the narcissist's reaction. Or the narcissist will triangulate with toxic words that tell you that your friends don't like you anyway, or they talk about you behind your back, or they said *this* about you, or that your parents/family/friends just use you. They will start arguments before family events, or before special occasions. When you arrive, they will be the life and soul of the party and leave you angry and frustrated. They can then use this against you further down the line when they make out that you are crazy.

When we are not isolated, we use our support system to help us see what's truly happening. When you have people saying things in the beginning, such as when the narcissist is treating you wrong and they think something is off, the narcissist will go all out to make sure you remove them from your life. Then, when you finally *do* see what is happening, our pride and guilt for not believing those who warned us, our fear of judgment, fear of being misunderstood, or embarrassment, makes us refrain from reaching out to these people who could help us. We are still with the narcissistic person, and they are usually masters of manipulation. They will have all your friends and family on their side and believe the them and not you.

Isolation is a red flag for future awareness when you start dating again. Try reaching out to the friends and family that you have been isolated from. You can also reach out to support groups where others have also lived through it and they understand you. It will build your confidence and help you connect with people again and not feel alone.

You can also make some amazing online friends! You can then start getting back into the real world. You can use online support groups, and then eventually meet them in person—because real interactions are what you want and they will heal you. It is not easy to start, especially when you are dealing with levels of anxiety.

Codependents need to really know their triggers, so they really know about themselves. Think about how you are feeling. Reinforce to yourself that you feel all right, and whenever anxiety creeps in, keep telling yourself that you are safe now. Start by just smiling at people and it will get easier. The more you practice, the better you will be able to get there.

When codependents are surrounded by narcissists, they no longer feel in control of their lives, thoughts, or even feelings. The narcissist convinces you that they are the only one who understands you, cares about you, and loves you. It's hard enough to be feeling alone in the world and have your mind clouded by thoughts that are not yours, all now based on narcissistic reality of the person in your life, thanks to their toxic words. Yet the only person you have for reality checks is the very person who is making you feel how you do.

They then come at you with verbal attacks against your insecurities, claiming that you need help, or that no one will love you. When you are taken down mentally by these words, they settled deep into our minds. Our minds just give in, and we start to believe that something is wrong with us. They make you feel grateful that you have them in their lives. When they play nice and use words such as, "after all, I do everything for you", in reality, they are doing very little for you. They are making your lives a living nightmare.

While this is happening, we don't understand they are the ones that are taking us down. They are now more in control of our minds. The toxicity chips away at our confidence and self-worth, leaving us questioning our own instincts. They make us believe we are not lovable and should be grateful for narcissist's negative and toxic love. Once you do start to see what is truly going on, you can start putting reality back into your own mind, creating your own thoughts and thinking for yourself again.

Learning and understanding of this disorder can guide you toward feeling farther and farther from being crazy. You are just being manipulated by someone to feel that way so that they could keep control over you. Understanding those insecurities are actually your instincts speaking out. Even though at the time you didn't know what they were telling you, now you *know* your instincts are telling you something. Trust them, as they are usually right.

From one moment to the next, you are confused as to whether you are continually going to be walking on eggshells around them... tiptoeing around the landmine in case you set them off. In reality, it is not *you* that sets them off. It's who they *are*—they set themselves off. This doesn't make it easy.

In time, you learn to understand that both their good and nasty sides are a part of who they are, and it's all manipulation to get their own needs met. They don't care for other people's needs.

It's all to distort our reality and our perceptions of them. It is all to train our minds to behave how they want.

They need to be able to control others, as they don't truly know what they want out of their lives. They feed off others. No matter what you do, it will never be right. They cause fear in your mind to question your abilities, to fear opening yourself around others, and to be afraid of what people will think about us. They cause us to worry about offending other people, and to worry about what other people's reactions to us might be for just being ourselves.

When you re-learn or recreate yourself into acceptance for exactly who you are or who you want to be, or you rediscover yourself, you remove self-doubt from your mind with good intention. There is no wrong or right way to live your life. There is only your way. It's better to do your best then to do nothing at all. We are all survivors and we are all here.

Good people will work to understand you and forgive innocent mistakes. Those who don't are not the people for you. Anger is normal. While still sitting in anger, use it to motivate you to make you better and not bitter. As humans, we have natural coping mechanisms in times of need. We can turn to fight, flight, freeze, or fall. Most of us fall into at least one of these while involved a narcissist codependent relationship, you may go through all four.

These are vital human instincts to protect us and won't endanger you around the narcissist. We are unwillingly putting ourselves in danger. Our instincts know. Our natural coping mechanism knows. Yet we just can't see it due to their many manipulation tactics—such as silent treatment, provoking, blame-shifting, projection, and gas lighting. This leads to our natural defense mechanisms being constantly called upon, and over a prolonged period of time, it can be damaging to who we are.

Some of us may have fought back, but the manipulators twist this so that we doubt ourselves. They will provoke you to bring out the worst in you so they can blame it all on you, as you are a good, caring person. You then feel guilty and do all you can to make it up to them for what they did. When you realize what they did, it can make you angry, which makes you take flight.

You can walk away, or go into no contact mode, but most codependents find that this hurts as much as being on the receiving end of the silent treatment for disappearing acts. We all know it cuts deep, and we all have the empathy to care. You start feeling guilty, like you are turning into the same type of person that they are when you start saving yourself. But you are not! There is a massive difference.

A narcissist uses disappearing acts or the silent treatment to punish you. They don't care for you. They just want to cause you pain so that you beg and plead to end the emotional pain and give in to their demands. They make you believe it was your fault. It was never your fault. When the codependent does this, the manipulator is not hurting.

Freeze is when you pause, unable to move no matter how much you want to. Most of the codependents have been on the receiving end of the narcissist's cold, dark, and empty soul. When you look straight at it the first time, it sends shivers down the spine. Most of us freeze. You get a feeling that something bad is about to happen, and you just can't move.

Over time, this passes and some of us learn to snap out of it, or leave before they go out of control. Looking back, you might feel stupid for letting yourself get in that deep, for not walking away sooner. You can't change what you didn't know. This is not your fault. It didn't start or end with you. Sometimes, we just completely give up on ourselves, feeling depressed, anxious, and hurting and with nowhere to go and no one whom you can confide in, and you just do as you are told.

Most of the time you don't see or understand what's happening. It can be one moment, a light bulb when we start to rise. That moment when we realize that we need out and do our best to get out safely. Once you are out, it may calm your anger, or they may leave you and move on in their lives. They may drag families through the court and you can see that they are lying through their teeth, yet you are still hurting and healing.

So, we feel anger towards them for the way they are treating you, the way they treat the children, the fact that they simply do not care… anger towards ourselves that we didn't see it sooner than we did, and didn't leave when we should have. You start resenting everything because you start to feel that of all these years you spent with them were all based on lies. You feel resentment that they can seemingly just move on without a care in the world. They might still come at you with endless mind games.

Holding on to the anger, resentment, and all those negative thoughts and experiences keeps our minds locked in the past. When we don't truly let go and release all the pain, we carry the story through the present and into our future.

Chapter 3: Comprehension of Jealousy-Driven, Controlling Behavior

Nobody likes to feel that someone else is controlling their destiny or their everyday actions. One of the most recurring questions that clients talk about is, "How do they make a relationship work when the other person is being so controlling?"

Codependents can be either active or passive. Active are often confused with being narcissistic. However, both active and passive codependents have the common feature of being attracted to a narcissist. A passive codependent is a person best described as a character from a 1960's sitcom. He is quiet, meek, and is very afraid of causing trouble. They can be intimidated very easily. They try to satisfy their needs through a passive approach in their relationships. But because they are in a relationship with a narcissist, those needs are never met.

The passive codependent is the more sympathetic of the two categories. They present a saintly façade where they are always giving and patient, but they suffer silently. No one knows their true pain, because they are too afraid to express what a lot of people already recognize. That they are in a relationship with someone who is not able to meet their needs or has no motivation to fulfill their needs.

We watch them suffer, and wonder why they don't fight back. The passive codependent has more self-esteem issues than an active codependent. They are more fearful, easily dominated by the narcissist, and more susceptible to harm, abuse, and situations in which they can't adequately protect themselves or their loved ones.

The other type is the argumentative, or active codependent. They are the ones who are always following their narcissistic partner. They are always trying to control and watch over their partner. They involve themselves in fights and arguments. They try, albeit unsuccessfully, to control the narcissist partner.

To others who don't know them well, the active codependent actually looks narcissistic. A question that stirs confusion is, "How a codependent can be controlling and manipulative but not be narcissistic?" A codependent gives love, respect, and care to others but doesn't expect or get the same in return. The narcissist is the opposite personality who takes love, care, and respect from others and doesn't reciprocate.

The active codependent will fight to get their needs met, but ultimately, because they are in a relationship with a narcissist, they never quite get what they need. They try to control, they fight and manipulate, but at the end of the day, they stay in a relationship with a person who can never meet their love, care, and respect.

The active codependent can spend their whole relationship with the narcissist and never leave. That is the difference between a healthy person and an active codependent. A healthier person might use control and manipulation to stop a person from hurting them, but when they finally realize that their feelings will never be reciprocated, they end the relationship. The active codependent, because their self-esteem levels are similar to that of a passive codependent, doesn't feel strong or secure enough to end the relationship.

Usually, when an individual tries to control another person and acts and feels in charge of the other person's actions, the most typical reaction from the suffering party is rebellion, but it is not always immediate or overt. Sometimes people live in a situation of being controlled for a long period of time, all the while developing deeper resentment. They end up becoming frustrated with the controlling partner, as well as with everyone else they know.

Two things are going on in a controlling relationship—the first is the thought, "No matter what you say, nothing is ever going to be different. I am angry and I don't anticipate any kind of future that can be better. I want out of this!"

The second is the insistence of the other person that, "No matter what you say, I am not controlling at all." You can never tell the controlling person that they are controlling, because they will never accept it. It is important to talk at a time when the discussion is not event driven. When you discuss heavy emotions when an event is occurring, there is an emotional disconnect from the other person. When you wait until your discussion is not event driven, you can connect on a more emotional level, and the other individual is less likely to get defensive and stop listening.

There is a much better chance of communication if it starts from a place of feeling, rather than attack: "I feel as though I am not in control, and as though my actions are being called upon from someone/something outside of me..." instead of directly making an accusation of controlling behavior. It allows the other person to examine behavior from a more peripheral, wide point of view, rather than remaining in a tunnel vision viewpoint that is often felt when we are under attack. This is also where a therapist can bring an outsider's perspective into your relationship and really define the dynamics of what the nature of the relationship is between the parties, and help generate awareness in both their minds about what is going on. You can't *be*ware until you are *a*ware.

One of the most common reasons that people try to control another individual is out of fear that you are going to hurt them. It often comes in the form of constant advice, nagging, or pursuing something in someone's life. They never admit that they are trying to control others, they say they are helping them.

You need to understand self-determination. This says that you want to be able to make your own decisions about what you do, what you eat, where you go, or what you think. When it comes to children, you can only allow a little self-determination, because they don't have much knowledge to use as a basis for understanding. As they grow, they develop more and more into making their own decisions based on what they feel or what they want to do. It boils down to them wanting to be trusted like an equal.

The controlling person never perceives the behavior as a negative thing. They perceive it to be an acceptable behavior, and when they receive negative responses to it from the suffering party, they think it is coming from a place of disagreement with them and wanting different things which they perceive as wrong. This leaves them with feelings of rejection. In reality, the one being controlled is just trying to steer clear of anything negative from the controlling partner.

When we feel as though we are being rejected, and someone is not open to receiving what we are trying to say, we feel dejected. It is very easy to transition into a mental thought of we are not good. If the person who is feeling controlled is trying to build a healthier relationship, this is something they need to avoid making their controlling partner feel.

In order to move to a place where we can build a positive emotional influence or connection, we need to give value to that human. You need to remember that they may feel as though you are starting to devalue them. You need to speak up. It won't get better on its own. When you do speak up, you may want to add more to *how* you feel rather than what you *think* they are doing. You need to come from a place where you are not attacking the other person, but rather, are speaking from your perspective and feelings. This will help them not go into attack or defend mode, and help them try better to understand your viewpoint.

Chapter 4: How Can Codependency Ruin Relationships?

Codependents lack a healthy sense of self. They are ultimately lost within themselves. They are prone to put others first rather than have their own needs fulfilled. Codependents are the people who have trouble accessing their internal cues, and so they think and behave differently around another person.

This includes people who are addicts, or processes such as sex addiction, gambling, or substance abuse—such as food disorders—or any other kind of addiction. The need to use or consume starts with the feeling of emptiness and damage done in childhood, often concealed by a sense of devalued self, shame, emotional abandonment. Children adapt to the environment in different ways in order to survive, and one of the ways to soothe yourself is to adapt to other people.

In this case, their thinking and behavior begins to revolve around another person, similar to how some teenagers might turn towards substance or video addiction. It used to be music. Now it's gaming, internet, and phones. They use it to soothe themselves because of the pain, anxiety, depression, or whatever is going on internally.

The Development of a Codependent

This is the same way, and for many of the same reasons, that someone who is codependent turns toward another individual. When a child is raised by parents lack empathy and mutuality, they will try to make themselves visible to the adults, and attempt to find out what will keep them safe. They discover whether they need to achieve or please, depending on the child's personality.

The more the codependent goes through these changes in order to survive their own emotional selves, whether in the form of using drugs or adapting to someone else, the larger the gap becomes between their real self and codependent self. They eventually develop a default zone. It can be a pleader, a rebel, hero of the family, or any such role that they may develop. That becomes their personality. Maybe they are always trying to tell jokes, whether to distract their parents from fighting or make them laugh. The more the person does this, the farther they get from their real selves. Authenticity becomes a distant memory.

This has much to do with their levels of neglect or punishment when they were growing up. Even well-meaning parents, who may not have been overtly abusive, can sometimes use shame tactics with their children by being intense. Similar to physical violence—sexual abuse can also play a role.

There is a phenomenon called the trauma of images of invisibility. Children will ask the adult about their childhood and think it was fine. They remember going on vacations, and that they had everything they needed. They went to good schools, but their parents existed in an emotional vacuum. In this case, a void develops and children don't get the closeness and emotional attachment that they need to thrive. They learn to not turn to their parents for comfort, or even when they are feeling distressed.

These parents are often well meaning, they are just too busy with each other, work, financial stress, or any other reasons they may have. But their actions, even unintentional, can cause a child to start to feel ashamed of their feelings, which are very integral to who we are as a human being. To become a whole individual, we form an identity with our own individual thoughts and feelings, perceptions and beliefs. We are able to become an asset—distinguishing us from what our parents want, and their beliefs in their raising of us.

This is called the individuating. We become separate. If parents are depressed and codependent, they may even raise their children to become codependents. Because their parents aren't emotionally available, they are unable to meet their needs.

Shame doesn't come into play as an emotional concept until you are over a year old. There are different studies where some say that it isn't until after a child three years old, where may show disgust, or their bowel movements may change. These are signs.

Babies are forming their relationships and emotions, but most people don't think of babies as individuals. They are, and they form their identity in relation to someone else. Just like therapy is a process based on the reaction from another person so we can heal our identity in a relationship with somebody else. People have a lot of cognitive distortions. Because of perceptions are usually formed by what we are taught, or what we experience, the result often comes from faulty parenting.

When a parent is raging at a child, they come to believe that they are a terrible child. Maybe parents aren't even saying anything, they are just being busy on their phones. This can cause the child to become emotionally distant. It is absolutely necessary to tell your children, and help them believe that they matter to both their parents. They need to feel and understand that each parent wants a relationship with them, and not just because they are performing well in school or they are soccer stars, but for who they authentically are.

Children shouldn't be turned away from when they are crying, or think that they are bad because their parents are angry. Parents need to make them feel that they are accepted, and that their parents honestly want to spend time with them. It is only by demonstration that a parent creates a child's interest in values. It's good to have it coming from one parent, but still, it's not enough, because it creates trauma in his mind when he doesn't have it from both of his parents.

Sometimes when one sibling gets more attention than the other, the one left out may start to feel more like an outsider in the family. This can also happen when the parents are fair, but their siblings are narcissistic. They may be teasing them, abusing them, or even physically hurting them, and parents are at fault for not intervening and not protecting them. This again makes the child think that there's something wrong with them.

Enter Codependency

Codependency can be thought of as a secondary condition. It's really a symptom of deeper problems. When we evaluate codependency, it is not the problem itself that we treat, but rather a problem that is caused by something much deeper. Therapists are better equipped to work to solve the problem. Codependency is a product of not only deep shame, but more along the lines as a response to trauma. The type of trauma is called attachment trauma. It occurs during the early years of one's life, during the time when they are bonding with their parents.

Children of narcissistic parents observe and do what makes their parents happy, and ultimately get some semblance of what they want. But what they don't get is the feeling of self-worth. They start to experience a sense of deep loneliness. They develop a relationship template that is about giving to others in order to feel love or comfort in one's own skin.

That relationship template is then taken and is manifested into codependency. At the very core of a codependent is the sense of loneliness. It is deeply painful. It burns with pain. The only way that the codependent can often find love is with a narcissist. They find that this style of relationship takes away the loneliness and makes them feel comfortable. The codependent feels complete.

In reality, this is really a relationship comprised of two underdeveloped people. It can be referred to as half-person relationship, because they need each other to feel good, to feel whole. That's why their relationship starts up so quickly, intensely, and often sexually. In order to feel complete and whole in the world in which they live, they need to connect to another person.

The codependent who needs another person to feel good about themselves is usually either battling, or running away from, toxic levels of loneliness. Talk to any codependent, and they will tell you that outside of a relationship, the feeling of intense loneliness becomes something that cannot helped but be focused upon.

This loneliness can often be traced back to attachment trauma. But the codependent avoids the loneliness by becoming attracted to the narcissist. Even though it is dysfunctional, the loneliness is held at bay. When they are facing a situation of leaving the narcissist, the narcissist leaves them, or they should be alone, they fall back into feeling lonely. This loneliness is their number one withdrawal symptom. Codependency is like an addiction, because to feel real euphoria, a codependent needs a relationship with a narcissist. They feel like they have a place on this Earth. They belong to someone even though that person is troubled.

Chapter 5: Warning Signs of Codependency

The questions you need to be asking yourself is whether you feel stuck in your relationship? Or invisible? Or whether you feel dissatisfied? If so, there is a possibility that you are in a codependent relationship.

A codependent relationship can be simply described as an attachment to the idea that you need something outside of yourself to validate you and make you feel real, seen, or to feel worthy. Most psychotherapists believe codependency is the result of childhood abuse such as neglect, abuse by omission, or abuse by the commission of overt abuse or covert abuse. There are various ways codependency manifests itself in a relationship. This checklist can help you to really understand the signs that you may be a codependent person.

The codependent seeks validation outside of the self. They often feel like victims and stuck in their current living situation.

They are secretly angry or secretly depressed. They don't like talking about what they are feeling to anyone.

They may experience brain fog, where they feel disconnected from those who surround them.

They settle for whomever shows up, or any person who likes them.

They ramble on without thinking. They react rather than act on their own.

They wait for others to give them permission to feel worthy. They feel they are unworthy.

They look for others to fix them. They may tend to trap others into taking care of them. This is due to the fact that they don't know how to take care of themselves.

They may have sex when they don't want to. They may seem to have difficulty in enjoying sex.

They don't have dreams. They often wonder why others are happy and they are not.

They trust too easily. They are easily wounded. Other peoples' struggles affect their serenity. They focus their mental strength on solving others' problems or relieving their pain.

They focus their mental attention on pleasing others and trying to protect others.

They feel invisible. Sometimes they are over-reactive and sometimes they are under reactive. They judge themselves too harshly. They think everyone hates them. They obsess about trying to be good enough.

They are worried they will never experience true love. They feel ashamed because their parents failed to love them unconditionally and authentically.

They feel guilty when they say no. They suffer from bulimia, anorexia, or may struggle with drugs or addictions. They seek distractions.

They have constant anxiety. They have trouble sleeping or may oversleep.

They have trouble identifying their feelings and fail to know the difference between thinking and feeling.

They understand everyone else but themselves. They don't know who they really are. They have no sense of self.

They fear abandonment and intimacy. They are children in adult bodies.

Our society is infused with varying ideas of codependency. As individuals, we need to awaken and realize how we are being manipulated from outside forces, such as we are seeking validation from outside of ourselves. When we are never actually getting any, we can't develop a healthy sense of self. We can't have self-esteem if we don't have a developed sense of self, and if we lack self-esteem, it makes us prone to self-loathing, anxiety, and other various mental issues.

One of the major troubles concerning this issue is a lack of awareness. People who are codependent find it difficult to rationalize their behavior because they don't know why they are feeling what they are feeling. This lack of knowledge makes them feel they are going crazy. They give into the powerlessness of their minds, and begin to think there is something wrong with them. However, it is just a reaction of the mind and body to being codependent. These signs need to be carefully checked and resonated with your life to know whether you are a codependent or not.

Codependency is the need to be needed. We're not just talking about feeling good when needed, but absolutely *needing* to be needed, especially by our significant other. But sometimes we find that our identity is based on being needed by other people. It is a blurring of the boundary between healthy and unhealthy dependence. It becomes codependence when we *need* to be needed.

You think that all you are bringing to the relationship is your ability to fix your significant other, to be able to solve theirs or other people's problems. You feel that the survival of the relationship depends on you, and rests on your shoulders. You feel hurt and resentful when people aren't praising you and recognizing you for whatever you are doing because you are doing a lot and giving a lot. You end up feeling ripped off and taken advantage of, or taken for granted when people don't recognize your efforts.

You may need to feel in control at all times. You need to avoid conflict of any kind, and will do so at any cost. You are willing to do anything, give in, put your stuff aside, and act in ways that you are not even comfortable with just to avoid conflicts.

The thought of conflict brings up severe fear and pain, because you feel that if there is conflict in the relationship, and you do or say something that the other person doesn't like, they might leave you. There is a fear that they don't have any use for you. You fear being unable to fulfill their needs. You feel like you will be stripped of all your value and ultimately end up alone. You have a hard time trusting your own self. You constantly fear that if you make a mistake people are going to abandon you.

This is codependency at its hardest.

Part 2

Chapter 1: Stages of Codependency

It's important to begin by knowing that people seeking codependency recovery can experience a lot of negative situations. To illustrate... if you smoke, the Surgeon General warns that you can get lung cancer, heart disease, emphysema, it may complicate pregnancy, and you will probably die early. This is a proper warning which gives the person the choice, or an opportunity to make a choice, as to whether they want to be a smoker or not.

Similarly, if you continue on this path of codependency recovery, a lot can happen. You may experience the worst emotional psychological pain that you have ever experienced in your life. So, you need to be prepared to embark on this challenging journey of revisiting past trauma. This warning is therefore very important, as it helps you to participate in the cost-benefit proposition. You may choose whether or not you want to pursue this. It creates realistic expectations.

Especially in the initial stages of codependency recovery, there is going to be a lot of resistance and negativity that may cloud your mind. It is important to generate awareness about that. This information can motivate and inspire you, as well as realistically prepare you to face this disorder. Once you resolve to do this, you are going to get rid yourself of all your adversaries. The warning starts with a set of factual information on what happens when you decide to no longer subjugate yourself to passivity. You make the decision to no longer be in invisible relationships. It is fine to feel scared. But you should know if you are really set to get out of this cycle, it is going to be difficult.

For example, after a hip replacement, one suffers a lot of pain and may not want to go to the doctor for another hip replacement. Being in surgery does hurt and it will be complemented by recovery, and the need to undergo physical therapy. If you want to quit, you might even die if you refuse it. But if you go through it, after a short while, the positives of the surgery are going to pay off.

At the initial stage, when there are fear and anxiety, everyone goes through it. Even though it is difficult, the payoff is worth it. It is very necessary to learn how to change your propensity to always finding yourself attached to the wrong person. Codependents tend to get into relationships with narcissists and addicts.

It's important to understand the nature of the problem, and approach it like you approach an addiction. There are four accurate stages of codependency recovery. Each stage has a particular time span. However, no one individual stage is the same.

STAGE ONE:

Stage one may last for five to six months for some, or it can take up to a year to get through this first stage.

Begin with a zero-step, in which you acknowledge that you have a problem. It may be hard to admit, but you need to realize and accept that you have a problem and there is an actual name for the problem. This leads you to seek help. This gets us to stage one.

The first stage is setting boundaries. In therapy, this stage is when the client decides they are ready. It's time for them to change the psychological landscape of their life. Their therapist has gone over all the risks of getting into the program.

The first stage is spread over a zero to three months range. It is the most difficult and challenging stage of all. It is analogous to being an alcoholic and quitting alcohol. It could be like any addictive drug that has a difficult withdrawal syndrome. It is extremely anxiety-provoking.

People in this stage are scared to death to deal with depression and panic because they have worried their whole life about what would happen if they finally set boundaries. Several clients have never set boundaries with their loved ones in their entire lifetime. To set boundaries is scary because loved ones can become up in arms and extremely angry. They experience these boundaries as an attack upon them.

Codependents are reflexively and magnetically attracted to narcissists. One is a caregiver and the other is a care-taker. They both fit perfectly in this functional relationship that requires their opposite personality to keep them together.

But when you break free from this dance and you challenge the person by disagreeing with them, the narcissist tends to not have the ability to accept fault in the problems. They tend to get very angry and feel betrayed, and they move toward blaming the person who is blaming them. They fail to see what's wrong with themselves, but can always see what's wrong with others.

In stage one, when you are setting boundaries for the first time, this is the first time that you stand up to the narcissist. It is the time to insist that he or she do something that they would normally do to you, such as saying to your partner, "I am going out with the girls today," or ask them to take the children to the swimming classes.

The narcissist is always going to be very angry with this reversal. They can be threatening, whether overt or covert, and they may use anger or emotional manipulation. This can be very scary for the codependent because they have never really experienced safety in speaking their truth. The aggression or passive aggression of the narcissist is something they have avoided standing up to their whole life.

Another important thing to keep in mind in this stage is the possibility of immediate loss of friendships and relationships. Both the people who love you and people who don't love you are all going to be angry. Even though this sounds silly, it is a fact. You won't be able to tell the difference. There will, however, be a separation of two in the latter stages.

Your children may be enraged. You will tell them to leave their phones and laptops and come to the table to have dinner for the very first time. You have set a boundary. They will treat you like you are a stranger. They may look at you with hatred. You will very quickly learn what happens when a codependent sets boundaries and reasonable expectations. It immediately seems like the world is going to explode.

So, you need to be ready for the loss of friendships and relationships, and you can never know for sure whether they can be reconciled or not. If you worry about losing relationships in stage one, it counteracts with all of the processes and tasks necessary in this stage.

It's important to manage these moments when you just feel like caving in. You can't say, "Enough is enough. I can't manage the constant threats and manipulation." You need to go ahead full force with the narcissist, and any other person in your life, who want you to remain the codependent that you always have been.

You are going to feel isolated. You will deal with criticism and condemnation. You are going to be told paradoxically and unfairly that you are being selfish. Even though it is a very sad accusation to the codependent who has always been selflessly connected to their loved ones. They have done everything for everybody.

The moment they set boundaries; they are called selfish. The reason why the emotional manipulators say these things is because it has always worked on the codependent before. Dating back to their childhood, if someone told them that they are going to become a person who is either a codependent or selfish, it has always enticed the codependent to back down and meet the needs of the emotional manipulator.

This stage will last for about three months, and a therapist needs to focus on keeping the codependent strong and motivated. They have to help them manage the compulsion to give up or give in.

STAGE TWO:

This is where the intensity of the conflict comes down a few notches. It is still a very difficult stage. Stage two is about maintaining boundaries in a hostile environment. You have already set boundaries for the things you will or will not do anymore. You have spent two or three months with people being very angry, threatening, and trying to be manipulative to get you back to your codependent ways. But you have been strong and you believe that you deserve to be loved and cared for in an equal proportion that you do for others.

In this stage, those who don't love you, whether they are your spouse, best friends, or people you have known your whole life—even family members, they start to go away. This process is like separating the wheat from the chaff. This is when the narcissist can't tolerate a relationship that is balanced to some degree of mutuality and reciprocity. They decide that they can't be in a relationship like that and leave. The recovering codependent moving beyond stage one starts to hold fast to their boundaries and the relationship ends.

It is a very difficult stage because relationships that you thought were loving and caring just break down. It becomes a daunting experience when the people whom you nurtured were only good as long as you were taking care of them, and as soon as your codependency stopped, the relationship fails to persevere. The narcissist goes away. This is when the codependent may need to begin grief work. The indignant unreasonableness of breaking off the relationship by the narcissist hurts the codependent, and this is what this stage brings about.

Imagine that suddenly your parents, after you stopped being codependent, ask you to stop seeing them. It brings in a lot of grief. Compared to stage one, where the withdrawal symptoms are high, this stage it is not as high. However, the temptation to leave these new ways and move back to old ways can be intense.

It is really necessary to delineate between healthy and narcissistic relationships. This is the stage where we are learning what is acceptable and what is not. It is not all or nothing. It is not possible to get rid of all the narcissists and only keep the loving, healthy and balanced people. That's unreasonable and unrealistic.

The questions that arise are, "What is fair?", "What level of reciprocal mutuality is acceptable?" and, "How much empathy am I willing to give up?" The codependent needs to acclimate to the narcissist's slung injuries, guilt trips, shaming, and allegations of being selfish.

Once they get accustomed to it, they can start to predict it. They start to feel more confident, have fewer negative thoughts and fears, and over time, they become more and more confident. They set their boundaries without the fear of someone not wanting to be in a relationship with them.

Before their recovery, the codependent would not set boundaries because of the fear of being alone. In stage two, the boundaries are set because they know that having a healthy relationship is far more important than the anxiety, fear, and grief in these stages.

STAGE THREE:

This stage lasts for over 6 months. It's longer than the previous stages. The first stage includes everyone being angry. You doubt whether this is the right decision, and you struggle with finding whether it's worth it.

Stage two is separating the wheat from the chaff, where you start to experience people disappearing. You maintain your boundaries and hostile environment but eventually, over time, the smoke clears. In the time of building relationships and experimenting, this is the stage of dissolution for the codependent and narcissistic relationship experience.

The codependent no longer feels codependent. They no longer accept others unfairly, like expecting more from a person than what they are willing to give. Their anxiety and fear of being lonely start to lessen. They start to experiment and reach to those who are around. They start to build upon new relationships or reconfirm some older relationships. Family members may get over what they unfairly perceived as selfishness.

There are a few people who threaten to leave the codependent in stage one. At this stage, some of them return. It doesn't mean their narcissism has disappeared. It just means that they have accepted that this person who now has more self-respect, sets boundaries, and are a pain to their inner narcissist—but they still want them in their lives. This comes to show the recovering codependent that they are more important to them.

It is usually very satisfying to clients in stage three, when they find out how people come back to them, who once promised and threatened never to see them again. This new relationship brings more mutuality and sharing. The recovering codependent experiences the support and respect that they may have never experienced in their whole life.

This can be termed as reconfiguring human magnetism. We, as humans, are magnetically drawn to others... such as a codependent to a narcissist, and the same as a healthy person to another healthy person. A healthy person who is loving and caring may find themselves attracted to someone who is bold and a little bit self-centered. This is the reconfiguration of attraction patterns. You may find that you are no longer attracted to narcissists.

In this stage, you talk about what it's like to date someone who listens. The excitement of some of my clients who start experiencing conversations and associations with people who really listen to them and reciprocate with kind and polite things is surreal. If things don't go right and the narcissist resurfaces, the codependent can detach themselves easily. They are not pulled into the drama that the emotional manipulators subject them to. They spot it and they set a boundary. When it doesn't work out, they remove themselves, because they have had a practice of about six months to a year.

Their painful episodes of loneliness are less frequent. Loneliness is key with withdrawal symptoms of codependency recovery. In the first stage, the codependent faces deep bouts of loneliness that are painful. Those bouts are now gone. Sometimes being lonely even feels good.

In stage three, just like any addiction, there can be some relapses. Sometimes the codependent can lose their judgment, has a bad day, or something goes wrong and they relapse. They may go back to a lover. But they quickly bounce back, because they can't fall back into the cycle. They realize the progress that they have made, and that relapsing is not an acceptable proposition.

STAGE FOUR:

This is the last stage, which lasts for more than a year. At this stage, your relationship orientation has taken roots, and you are essentially focusing on reinforcing and strengthening the relationship. It is an exciting time, especially for the therapist, to see that their client is finally finding a happy place, and are in love with people who share and love as much as they do.

There is a complete cessation of pathological caretaking. The relationships that they have are mutually loving, respecting, and caring. It doesn't mean that it's equal all of the time. No one has ever experienced any relationship equally. You just have to find a balance.

The new relationships will be defined by a fair distribution of love, and healthy boundaries that are open and go both ways. There is going to be interdependence. Interdependence means they are separate, but connected. It means to have your own individuality, but also be connected in a relationship. Interdependence and reciprocity in any healthy relationship are of the utmost importance.

In this stage, your loved ones will admire and affirm your growth and change, unlike stage one where everyone is angry. All of a sudden, you find that people are admiring you. The people who criticized the recovering codependent in stage one and two for being selfish, start to say how much healthier and stronger you seem. The critics have forgotten their complaints and feel closer to you.

Relationships are balanced, and cravings and withdrawal symptoms have dwindled or stopped. Now the codependent is repelled by a narcissist. There is almost a reflexive reaction when they are in a situation with a narcissist. They are immediately turned off by narcissists, and turned on by healthy perspective partners.

Chapter 2: How to Overcome Codependency

There is a technique called observe and don't absorb. It is the technique that helps the onslaught of manipulation that happens in stage one. It is influenced by a saying by George Bernard Shaw where he said, "Never to wrestle with a pig. You get dirty and besides, the pigs like it."

In other words, the codependents always lose the fight with their emotional manipulator. When they start wrestling with the proverbial pig, they will always find themselves more powerless and disadvantaged. The emotional manipulator thrives on control and power. He wants to pull the codependent into their conflict because that is where he knows how to change or influence people, and how to get them to back down and allow himself to get what he wants.

Codependents have to learn when they are brought into the narcissist's world it is analogous to ingesting toxins. They need to think of it as a toxic environment, because they may tend to lose their emotional control and their perspective of self-care. The 'observe and don't absorb' technique allows the codependent to maintain control.

The technique tells you to artificially detach from the narcissist. You need to observe the narcissist, which prevents them from connecting to you effectively or emotionally. But when you absorb, you are participating in this dysfunctional dance in which you have lost control and are not in an environment in which you can defend themselves and set boundaries. Therefore, it can be termed as conscious, or healthy, disassociation. It is a purposeful emotional detachment. It helps to neutralize their power and control.

These are a few tips that you can follow to completely use observe and don't absorb technique. First, you need to remember the saying we discussed earlier on. When you are able to practice observing, it gives you the home-field advantage.

Pretend to be an observer while interacting with an emotional manipulator. If you disconnect and see it from an observational point of view, you will no longer be dependent on them. You will be able to clearly see how dysfunctional they are. You will render them incapable of manipulating you if you don't react to what they want to project on you.

Imagine that you are looking at an instructional video about the narcissist. As you watch, really watch for the typical symptoms of their behavior. Pay attention to the strategies they use to pull you into the fight. Look at them from head to toe. Watch their facial reactions and body posture.

The more you see them as individuals with psychological problems, the more you can step outside of the reaction to them. In real-time, you should be able to predict what he or she is trying to do now to get a certain reaction out of you. You need to tell yourself that you are strong and in control and continue saying it.

If you absorb, you will fall prey to their manipulations and become a victim. They will control you. But if you observe, you won't get upset and your boundaries will remain solid. You must keep your tone and volume even, and breathe deeply. Stay connected to your body. If you let go of this control, it will bring back stress, a wave of anxiety, and bring the toxins in.

Emotional manipulators create codependent children. It usually goes back to one of their parents or guardians being a narcissist. Whether they were an antisocial narcissist, an alcoholic, or a drug-addict. The parent or guardian neglected the child's basic needs. They had this child either on purpose or by accident because they wanted to fulfill a fantasy. They wanted to create a life different from the life that they experienced. They wanted to be a nurturer or giver of life as a loving, caring parent because they did not experience it.

These very damaged parents see their child as a way to heal their wounds, to right the wrongs of their childhood, and love their child as they have never been loved. The problem is that the emotional manipulator is inherently damaged. They have serious psychological issues, unresolved trauma, and they really can't ever go beyond their own needs. They neglect or abuse the child.

This later decides whether this child will grow up to become a narcissist or a codependent. Neglecting the child makes the child realize, and it can be as early as still in infancy, that they will have to learn how to make their parents happy.

Whether it is by cooing, smiling, or not crying so much.

The future codependent adapts the learning to please. Pleased emotional manipulators want to care for their children. They feel competent, whole, and motivated to love their child because it is the child who never cries and always smiles, will go to sleep on time, and makes them feel good. They get to act out their fantasy of being this perfect parent.

But what the parent doesn't understand is that the love that they say they have for their children is conditional. A child instinctively, before he is even able to understand his environment, knows that if they are a pleasing child, they will get what he needs from his mother. So, the real love that this baby gets is conditional, and plays a major role in turning them into a codependent adult.

Successful adaptation for this future codependent child requires the child to learn the conditions of their life. They need to learn how to respond quickly and accurately to the demands of their parents. They develop a radar for the oscillations of moods—to know when mother or father is drunk, to cry more or to cry less, to not seem so needy. So, at a very early age, a child can have conscious thoughts. They use their hypervigilance to be able to negotiate in their mind when to seek what they need—and when not to.

Therefore, the infant grows into a child, learning how to not trigger the emotional manipulator, understanding their different moods, avoiding rage at all costs, and can stay away from neglect, abuse, or harm. Every child should have an opportunity to be whomever they are. The child in this situation feels that if they are not pleasing their parents, they suffer from loneliness, pain, and hunger. They become good actors. Going through adolescence and becoming adults, they learn to pretend to be happy even when they are not. Sometimes you can recognize these children.

If you know a narcissist or an alcoholic, their child keeps constantly looking at them. They can't be themselves without checking on their parents to find out whether it is safe. They become actors in their own life. Being agreeable and happy gets their needs met. They become experts in delaying their gratification.

They learn to suppress, control, and sublimate their emotions, because if they express these emotions, they find that their parents are not there when they need them. When they are hungry, no one feeds them, they stay in bed for too long, or their father doesn't play with him. They know through experience what works out to their disadvantage. When they annoy their parents and trigger a narcissistic injury, the next thing you know, the child is hurt and alone, both physically and emotionally.

They have learned to control their instincts to get what they need, and behave in a way that pleases their parent. They maintain the identity of a fantasy child. They help their parent maintain that persona of the fantasy. They learn to distort reality and comply with unnatural expectations.

The child is in this training ground that starts at birth and goes up to adolescence where they learn to control, subjugate, and repress emotions that potentially could be dangerous. They learn to be calm when frightened, happy when angry, and lovable in unlovable situations. Survival for this codependent requires a chameleon-like ability to blend into their environment, to know when it is important to be noticed and when you should not be noticed.

If you are a child of a narcissist you don't want to take away too much attention from your parents. You don't want to cause negative attention, because that will only cause anger, upset, and potentially rage in the parent. They must know when they need to be seen and when not. These kids who are so obedient and so successful in school or at dancing or baseball— it's all to just please their parents. They get so much attention because they are the best at what they do, or they are cutest and most adorable child... and they are doing it just to keep their parents happy. They are forced to mature before their time.

You can't effectively love anyone if you don't love yourself. Codependents don't understand how often they usually dissociate, why they disassociate, and how that affects their recovery today. The acknowledgment that to survive as a child or an adult they have to turn off their feelings... disconnect from their feelings and memories to stay sane and normal.

A codependent remembers everything bad that happened to them because they walk around with a lot of pain and suffering. People disassociate from their feelings completely to escape the pain of not being loved, or the pain that you don't belong. They may develop a tough exterior, but be completely numb on the inside. This continues to your adulthood where you aren't connected to how *you* feel and are connected to how *others* feel. It is so much easier and safer to know how your spouse feels, or your mother feels, than to know how you feel.

Recovering codependents and codependents, in general, learn that if they should recognize the unfairness of the harm and neglect that they are experiencing, they will get angry. If they get angry and communicate it verbally or non-verbally. When the narcissist in their life sees it, they punish them. They punish them for being upset.

Either one can verbalize it or shut it down. That is where disassociation and disconnection of feelings and memories come in play. It helps the codependent survive, either as a child or as an adult. The brain associates with the pain, while at the same time expressing how they feel pleasure with shutting down. It's like a survival kit gone rogue. It is just not safe to feel anything. As an adult codependent, you are living this day in and day out without even realizing it.

Many times, a codependent starts to talk about what they feel, and then look at the narcissist, only to find that they are cut off and their faces go blank. They try to skate over what happened. Sometimes codependents can be so conditioned to not showing concern, that when they eventually try to, they are dysfunctional in expressing it.

If you are raised by your garden variety of narcissist, the psychological damage caused is severe because you are dealing with sociological elements of disorder. Being raised by a narcissist is a trauma in itself. There is a severe deficit in inner and outer reality. The inner reality doesn't match the outer.

For example, there was a preacher who had two daughters, both of whom were severely bulimic. In their childhood, they experienced emotional abuse where their parents forced them to go to church every day. The father beat up his wife and she did not tell anyone about this to save the family name. As kids, their mother was unable to protect them from this narcissist father. As a result, they started having sexual relations early on. One of them became pregnant too early, and ultimately brought a bad name to the family. Both were lacking in love, and developed severe eating disorders.

In this example, the children had this emotional gap from their father being loved by everyone, whereas they failed to see him as a good person. It creates so much confusion in the underdeveloped brain, and this is where a lot of disassociation comes from. The child can trust the internal experience of what's happening. Codependents learn that they are safe only when they focus on other people, and only when they can be there for their narcissists. They start projecting the personality type of a human doer, the invisible person. They are only loveable when they can take care of others.

Codependents assume that people can see through them to their imperfections and shameful secrets. That's where the ideal self comes in. The perfect version of ourselves is created to cope with our shame. The inner critic is the direct result of this phenomenon. Our inner critic insists that we conform to who it thinks we should be, and what it thinks we should feel. Since codependents can't function authentically, they organize their thinking and behavior around another person.

Take a personal inventory to see where your shame comes from. Look at the relationship pattern within your family origins. Consider what shameful messages you received as a child. Check their validity. Record what triggers your feeling of shame. Invent new responses to your shame triggers and practice anytime you feel ashamed. This can be a difficult process. You can do a lot of work on your own, although many people may even use counseling to help overcome shame.

Cognizance is the key to recover from codependency. It is consciousness or mindfulness. Self-awareness is the first building block to disrupting the negative behavior pattern. They are not fully grounded in the reality of the present moment.

Our decision making is impeded when we are not dealing with all the facts. Maybe the facts are being clouded by something else. Cognizance gives you immediate visibility into the reality of your current situation. It removes the barrier for you to be in tune with yourself.

You can become more adaptive to recognizing what's happening around you, such as manipulation, deception, or threats by other people. It lets you determine more calmly and clearly, whether a request from another person is valid or not. It tells you whether your urges should be acted upon, and where the boundary line should be in the circumstances you find yourself in.

Chapter 3: Are You Still Codependent?

It is possible to relapse into codependency no matter what recovery stage you are in the process of. When someone is in recovery from codependency, they may hit a problem in life in which they feel they can't or don't want to deal with. So, they get stuck. That can trigger a bit of a crisis, especially for someone who has been in recovery for a while.

The crisis may be the result of pride and not wanting to admit that there's a problem. Denial has kicked in again at that point, and that's a really big issue that can have a lasting effect on their recovery. This means that they are heading towards additional problems. In denial, they may start to use other things to distract... like painkillers, getting on the internet, playing games endlessly, or watching Netflix all weekend. These are examples of other ways of acting out to avoid your primary attention.

The trigger event may not even be that big. There can be a very small thing like a problem with your vehicle or a bill and it becomes a trigger for internal chaos. A very uncomfortable sense of self becomes a reality. Internal self-talk which is undermining in nature and physically painful to endure, becomes a habit. The dysfunction on the inside can only lead to dysfunction on the outside.

The old addict starts to resurface and they begin thinking that recovery is not going to work with the sort of person that they are. They become overwhelmed with the trigger and fail to comprehend the situation and let go of themselves. They start thinking about their pre-recovery times, the places they frequently visited, such as a favorite hangout place. They begin to use substances or develop problems in relationships... projecting stuff on other people, creating the crisis, etc., as a way of avoiding looking at themselves.

Substance misuse, food disorders, sexual issues... regardless of the choice of self-inflicted addiction, they lose further control. At some point, because they have been in recovery, they might reach a point of awareness of their actions and feel shocked, seeing it as a deviation from the steps they have been taking for their well-being. They may get back to a point of recognizing that they need help. That sort of brings back a shock to the system, and they restart the recovery process.

That's one route. The other route is the opposite extreme, where their behaviors continue to go on for some time, or the person may choose to end their life because they can no longer bear the shame and internal pain. There are various points in the relapse where you can pull yourself back and get into the recovery system. A relapse prevention plan is necessary, one that can chalk out the process that the person can adapt in case they are triggered.

Recovery makes codependents take charge of their lives as they're learning to value their feelings, needs, and opinions. As their self-esteem gets better, codependents find the determination to question their mistaken childhood beliefs. This then sets them free to know more about healthy relationship skills. This requires thorough practice.

Codependents normally fear that in their early recovery, they might become selfish. This is not true. Recovering codependents remain much more caring than most people. Recovery simply extends the abundant compassion of codependents towards themselves. They vow to become people respecters rather than people pleasers, and unconditionally respect their feelings and emotions.

To change a dysfunctional childhood, behavior, or beliefs takes practice, mindfulness, self-introspection, and time. The challenge to make such major changes comes from within. Life provides us with various opportunities to learn the lessons that we need in order to live a healthy, fulfilling and meaningful life. You need to know and understand that mental illness is not your fault. It is nothing to be ashamed of. It's a chemical imbalance and not personal.

Loneliness will always be a part of recovery, but it is a necessary part, because in truth, you are working on yourself, and no one can do that for you. Relapses can sometimes feel like the worst points in your life, because we often perceive relapses as failures. It is only a matter of changing your outlook on how you view these relapses. Even though you suffer greatly, you gain something from it. You gain empathy.

What is it Like to Live with Codependency?

Most of the time, you can't see on your own how much your loved ones care about you. When you take the steps to recovery, you discover what the illness is taking away from you, but you also see what you can gain from it. Finally, relapse is a crucial part of recovery. You may fall over and over again, but the important thing is to be *proactive* about relapse and not be *reactive* to it.

You need to stay vigilant and take care of yourself. Your relapses and struggles make you what you are. If you don't struggle, you don't find the true essence of your true self—like what your passions are. Relapses may occur in all areas of our lives. They can occur in your career, relationships, or society, in general. There can be a relapse in identity when you start to think that you don't know who you are anymore. Whenever you feel you have hit rock bottom, there is only one way to go, and that is up. You are going to get stronger and better.

There is a need for transformational behavior change. The underlying behavior of the codependent needs to be targeted and cured. They need to be taught and become well versed in regards to the gaps they had in their life, and the need to fill these gaps for a full recovery. They need to know they are capable of living their lives with integrity, accountability, and love for others. In order to be able to make a full recovery, and bid farewell to codependency, you have to follow a few simple steps.

The first step is to actually want to change. You need to keep in mind that life will get better when you leave your current situation and move to a healthier mind space.

The second step is to learn to act in a way where you are open to situations. It means that even if you don't want to be decent or codependent anymore, you act that way until it becomes you. You practice being a healthier person over and over until you become that person.

You know the kind of person you want to be like—perhaps how you don't want to get back into manipulating your partner, acting needy, etc. Envision yourself as already becoming that person. This is a very important step and action to take, and can't be achieved within a day. This practice needs to happen over a long period of time.

The next point to remember is to help others. When a person helps another, the helper becomes better. The way to save your life is saving another's life. You need to give responsibility to those who surround you, to hold you accountable for your actions. They need to be brutally honest with you when you mess up. This is where learning happens.

Sometimes when someone points out a fault in your behavior, you don't believe it to be true. If more than one person tells you the same, it will get you thinking. Recognizing your destructive flaws can help change you for a better person, when you are willing to accept and work on them. These people in your life are the ones who love and care about you and will want to see positive changes in you.

The next step is to have immediate consequences for bad behavior. Immediate consequences are necessary to your own expectations, so that you never feel it is right to come back to the pre-recovery stage.

Chapter 4: Heal All Your Relationships

You can stop the dysfunctional and generational patterns from continuing. You can end the legacy of abuse for you, your children, and all further generations. It's necessary to know that everything changes when the codependent gets healthy.

It's beyond just changing yourself, because it can change you, as well as people around you. You can stop attracting negative people into your life, and start to be truly happy again. Making lasting changes in our behavior is hard. The statistics are not very promising. Some studies show that 95% of all diets fail and only 8% of people keep their New Year's resolutions.

When in a relationship, you need to start asking questions. Are you interested in the outcome of your partner's work as if it were your own? This is a very specific way of being in a relationship. You are in a relationship with a person who needs saving. Making others happy is not your job. No one can make you happy and trying to do that for others would not do them any good either. It is such a seductive combination for a codependent to get in a relationship with a narcissist.

Narcissists and codependents are two halves of this perfect whole. The narcissist being the taker and controller, and the codependent who is a giver or a fixer—the person who wants to make everything right. Codependents focus on fulfilling all the needs of the narcissists, who are only concerned about fulfilling their own needs.

But there is something about this dynamic in the beginning. Narcissists are incredibly charming when they come in and sweep you off your feet. You feel a connection that you have never felt before in your life. They have the ability to make you feel like you are the only person in the room.

You are the perfect match for them. It is exciting to have this fast and furious relationship develop.

Once the narcissist really gets to know you and they know that they have you, the things you thought made you a perfect match start to go away. You get into a toxic cycle of being in a relationship where you have these peak moments, and then suddenly everything you do is wrong, you are being criticized all the time, and now you are working to gain that person's approval back.

Once you get the approval and you stick to the relationship, you will find yourself constantly trying to get their approval for one thing or another. There is no stability for this union. They both are trying to psychologically defend themselves. You are no longer handling core issues. You aren't solving your issues. It's equivalent to having a quiet agreement to work out your wounds, without getting a real resolution in the end.

A person with narcissistic qualities is always trying to hold a false sense of themselves, and they are not just doing this to show to the outside world. This is desperate attempt to avoid the insecurities and self-loathing they face in their lives. They want their narcissistic supply from the codependent. The codependent constantly feeds their ego and they get all of their needs met in that way.

No matter how much the codependent tried to adapt to what the narcissist wants from them, the narcissist needs to keep this cycle going. They will find a reason for the relationship to go bad again, in order to have the codependent to struggle to make it all good again.

The codependent is always being careful. They are constantly dialed into the narcissist's wants and desires. They feel overly responsible for the outcome of others. In this way, they avoid their own feelings and insecurities. There is superficiality in these relationships, because when they are acting out their wounds, they never get to a deeper level of intimacy.

How Do You Bring Boundaries into This Mix?

You increase awareness about yourself. You need to come to terms with… "How unhappy or happy, satisfied or unsatisfied, are you? How is it that you feel good? Or do you feel terrible?" You need to learn to focus on your own needs, even though you have been trained to not take care of yourself.

You need to recognize whether you are a hardcore codependent, or a high functioning codependent. A high functioning codependent is one who doesn't feel that they identify as being codependent. You can be a high functioning person who is working tirelessly to make a relationship work.

You need to get very honest with yourself, and reflect on what is happening in your relationships. What are you doing and how are you feeling? Then you observe yourself, without judgment, and take note of the way that you feel you need to deal with the people in your life who are your family, friends, or partners.

If you are codependent in the core relationship of your life, you are showcasing these codependent behaviors in your other relationships as well, and every relationship is impacted by this nature. This blocks you from anyone who wants to truly know who you are. It blocks a level of intimacy that you fail to have even in your friendships.

It may seem foolish to think that you need to dial into the questions of normal routine, such as being honest about what you wish to eat and how you want to act. And yet, it's an indication of a systemic way of being, and of you not prioritizing your preferences, pleasures, and desires. If you don't know what you really want, you won't be able to draw boundaries for yourself.

You need to then develop a harmless form of communication. Because it is hard for anyone who faces codependency, it is always appropriate to start with something positive. Instead of being rude and saying no, you may say, "Thanks for the invite, but we will plan something for the next time," and you can explain that you really appreciate that the other person thought of you.

It's completely your choice as to whether you want to provide the context of your decision, but always make sure that you are starting with positivity. Some people may resent you for being forthright with them, probably for the first time in your life. But if they genuinely love you, they will get past those feelings and return to your life.

Making lasting changes in our behavior is a battle. Most of us don't succeed at it for very long. When we discuss how we want to experience a good life, then lies the decision on how we utilize the ability to choose how we want to behave, and then follow through on it. Most of us think that when it comes to creating a new habit, it's a matter of willpower or discipline, and we don't have enough of either.

We might suspect inwardly that we are the kind of people who can't follow through on things. We think that this is beyond our comprehension and abilities to achieve. However, it is a skill. It is something that you can learn to do. You can get better at creating new habits.

The strategy to effectively heal and change your behavioral patterns is to start small. Most of us make the honest mistake of starting too big. We decide it is time to exercise and we go from not working out at all to being in the gym for an hour every day. You know what will happen. We may start out with good intention, but soon run out of steam, or maybe we are just unable to get off the ground. Maybe we start a two-week juice cleanse, and by dinner time we are eating a Domino's pizza.

Another example is to imagine that you are a critically acclaimed and literary award-winning writer. Then you sit down to write you a new novel—and nothing comes out. You sit for hours and days, and eventually months and years, of not being able to write at all. To cure this, we start small.

We start writing for five minutes a day. You may think that you are never going to get a novel done if you are only writing for five minutes a day. You may be right in thinking this, unless you have a very long life span. It's important to understand here that we procrastinate and avoid things that either feel overwhelming, or the task is too ambiguous. Writing a novel is both of those things.

By starting small, we can get going. One of the counterintuitive things about motivation is that it follows action. We always think it's the other way around. We get motivated then we take action. But this works in reverse as well. There are times that we can't think our way into the right action, so instead, we have to act our way into right thinking. In this way, the person can increase their momentum, increase their motivation, and consistency—and now start writing again.

Start smaller than you should, and do it every day. Focus on consistency. You will be surprised to see what a series of small steps taken every day can accomplish. As you proceed, the next step is to get into a self-improvement binge.

...We are not spending enough time with the kids. We are not eating right. Let's do an hour every day after dinner. We might even throw in the creative project that we have been putting off, and we will do it all today and every day for the rest of our lives...

Obviously, you know the repercussions of such a decision. What needs to be done is to focus on one part and make it happen. That part needs to get instilled in you, and become a part of you. Once that is embedded within you, you can make further improvements in life.

Don't change everything in your life at once. Pick one thing and get it down. Once you have integrated it into your life, you can build from there.

The final strategy is to make alliances with the right people. We forget to ask other people for help when we are trying to change. If you know anyone who knows what you are doing and is generally supportive, you are far more likely to make the changes that you envision to make in your life.

Having support from other people who are holding you accountable for what you are doing can be the difference between your success and failure when it comes to changing your behavior. These principles will apply to breaking your codependency habits and change the way you have been viewing relationships in life.

Chapter 5: Ten Step Program for a New Life without Codependency

Recognize That You Are Using These Behaviors to Cope with the Harms Caused to You

Codependents are victims, and we can trace that victimization all the way back to their childhood. That's where the client spends maximum time while undergoing therapy. The codependent needs to take responsibility for their disorder, because it hurts them by preventing them from ever loving themselves.

They need to take responsibility in how it has always prevented them from protecting their loved ones. Part of the denial system that keeps the problem alive is the belief that we are victims, we can't control others, and the best we can do is survive. This distorted thought process or cognitive distortion perpetuates the problem itself.

You are a partner to your own problem. Codependent parents harm their children. It's important to emphasize, that without accepting the fact that the disorder is harmful not only to yourself, but also to others, you can never really recover. The recovering codependent vehemently defend their parents, who were usually narcissist, in a semi-positive light. They need to be pushed into recognizing the reality—that their narcissistic parent was neglectful to their parental responsibility.

No one was capable of protecting them in their childhood from their narcissistic parent's harm. It is a tough pill to swallow and accept, that your parent who suffered from the disorder was themselves a co-conspirator to their own disorder, because of the fact that they were truly hurt as a child as well.

There are various bonafide reasons why parents suffering from codependent or narcissistic attributes couldn't leave their children so that they could grow in a healthier environment. But the codependents now need to search for what could have been done in those situations where the codependent parent sought help, and actively tried to protect their children.

What we often discover from this is that the parent who was suffering, had a fear of being alone. They had the same characteristics as their own parents—fear of being alone, tons of shame, pathological loneliness, inherent deficits and feeling of no personal power, lack of self-esteem, and troubled relationships with narcissistic people. This kept them locked into this weak victim's role. However, they could have changed.

If you don't first understand that your parent could have changed, they could have stood up for you, protected you, set boundaries, called the police, or threatened a divorce, there is no way you can get to apply that to your own life. If you continue thinking your parent kept doing the best they could, they had no choices, and you forgive them completely—there is nothing wrong with that.

When you start to discover through the therapy process that your codependency made you believe that you had few choices, made you believe you were trapped and had no power, and made you fall victim to the bullying, manipulation, and mind control, it helps the recovery process.

When we understand that the codependency disorder was a part of psychological perpetrator in keeping us in a victim's role, we know the problem that is to be resolved. What would have happened if their parents had done the right thing? You would have had a completely different life where you would have experienced self-love. You would have experienced a form of existential peace in an unconditional love and regard for themselves. Everything would have been different.

It is crucial for you to understand this basis for feeling. This is in no way an attempt to turn you against your parent. The purpose is not to get to mad at them. You may get angry because you have been in denial all these years. It is important for you to feel the feelings that are resurfacing whether it is anger, mad, or sad—or whatever they are—and then decide to let them go. You need to be honest to yourself.

Understand that you are a codependent because you were really hurt as a child. You are a victim of attachment trauma during the most crucial times of child development, and you did not feel safe to be yourself. Your parent was a narcissist and harmed you in a horrible manner. There may even be additional forms of harm, and your other parent who was a codependent did not protect you.

Understanding must be had here, as well. They did not protect you because they didn't know how to protect you. Secondly, they did not have enough love and self-esteem or care for themselves to do it. They were too afraid to stand up for themselves to protect their children. In the absence of protecting their children, they have given them this unconditional love, but the children still lived in a dysfunctional and unsafe environment.

If you want to eradicate codependency from your life, you have to look inside and understand the roots of it. You also have to accurately understand what your parents did to you, and not feel the need to sugarcoat.

Understand That Codependent Behaviors are Based in Shame

Codependency brings about a lot of confusion in our minds about what we are supposed to do and who we are as adults. It is very difficult, to tell the truth, to hold on to boundaries, to figure out what we think is fair or not.

We find it difficult to finish projects. It becomes daunting to correctly know when we should argue a point, and when it's inappropriate. Self is a podium that sits inside the heart space and most of us aren't even aware that we have a self. We don't realize that we are living in a constant state of reactivity. In an attempt to learn to live with our flaws because they are not us, it's the programming which is flawed, and we begin to understand why we feel ashamed.

A lot of it has to do with the fact that when you were young and you tried to reason with something, you may have been told that you were stupid. How can you come into a conversation with someone with such a strong personality? It becomes very difficult to be able to communicate what we think.

We have to know, before putting our point forward, about what they think and wrestle with the fear in our mind about what they would think about our view of the situation. You worry about what other people think about you when you are codependent. You worry about sounding stupid. You worry about other people taking extreme advantage of you. You are argumentative. You have to have the last word.

This stems from when the child has been picked on by their parents, brutalized by their siblings, and then they go to school and get bullied. We become adults, but our skin is so raw. We fail to realize that we are leaking energy and people who suck on the energy of others can pick up on that.

If you are highly sensitive and you have been bullied, it becomes easy to attract a narcissist. They know that you are easy to pick on, and it is fun for them to sit back and watch you react. You don't realize that you are actually attracting this attention due to your hypersensitivity. We are so worried that someone will take our power away, that eventually they do. Then we feel like victims, and they simply walk away, having made fools out of us.

There is nothing to be ashamed of. If you are programmed to feel what you feel, what other people think of you, what you thought was irrelevant, that your family has abandoned you—it becomes very hard to determine what we actually think. You are so afraid of being criticized and humiliated. There are families that lie about other family members. There are families where one parent is turning the entire family against one child, or there are families in which the only thing that their parents have in common is the disdain they have for their child. When this goes on in their homes, the children become codependent. We need to have our tribal instincts met. That sense of belonging is what we yearn for.

We wake up and realize that we have been thinking in a dysfunctional way, and there actually is a way to think in a healthy manner. It takes time and a lot of patience to be rerouted. You can change your brain by changing the way you think. The brain thinks the way it thinks because it has been conditioned to think so.

Unless you have really opened your mind up and questioned everything as a child, you will think how your parents made you think, depending on what the circumstances were when you were growing up. Your spirit knows when someone is being cruel, and it knows when you are lying. But the brain makes you feel afraid to tell your truth.

We lie because we are afraid of what people may think of us. We are unsure whether we have a right to think what we think. We are really afraid of being criticized. We lie because if we tell our truth, other people might get angry. We are afraid that we won't be liked. We never sit down and really become attuned to how we feel about what is happening around us. We are afraid to go there, because we don't know what to do when we decide that we are not happy.

If you are willing to face everything, your need to know what other people think about you doesn't matter. Your work is to deal with being in love with life, to look outside the window and see the trees and birds and see the sky—and to know that that lives within you. There is so much to be joyful about! When you learn this positive way of living, you start feeling that it's fine if someone doesn't like who you are. This is because you know who you are, and you like the person you are. People have their own realities and agendas.

People who are not very enlightened themselves are always projecting. They are in a state of reactivity. The more aware you become about yourself, the more you will be able to develop the quality to discern who is awake and who is not.

In the beginning, you may be surprised to see how a person may not even be capable of hearing what you are saying. When you reflect back on it and realize you were once bothered by this person's lack of sensitivity, it all becomes very clear. This will start happening to you as you move forward.

The truth does set you free. When you begin to tell the truth, you need to follow certain instructions. You can't get attached to an outcome. You can turn to your spouse and tell them that you want to go to marriage counseling because you feel that you both are codependent. That is your truth, and your truth can be that you really want both of you to feel connected and figure out what works best for you. But this may not be your spouse's truth. They may not want to be connected to you, or may not rank this as a priority, because they are way below the veil of consciousness.

Now what? It is important that we are not trying to tell our truth to hurt other people, or to manipulate them. You are not wrong for feeling a certain way. No one should dictate to you how to feel. But you need to be aware of your intention. Meditate daily to know how you feel, and really be in tune with your feelings. Stay in your reality, and what you feel is right, and observe the other person in their natural element. That's detachment.

Codependents don't detach. They stay meshed. You see your husband flirting with a waitress. When you react, they don't claim that they *aren't* flirting with the waitress, they say *you* are too sensitive. You are being insecure, and he was just joking around.

These are all excuses for not taking responsibility for their rude behavior. You just need to not react and stay quiet, rather than conversing with the person who literally has no respect for you. You should stay quiet at dinner or in the car. If they ask you what is wrong, it is up to you to either bring it up or leave it. You may then explain that it makes you feel uncomfortable when they flirt with waitresses.

If they deny it, remind yourself that in *your* reality he is doing that, and you have a right to feel the way you are feeling. Then you can ask them about how they feel about what you just expressed. If he is healthy, he will acknowledge his actions, and apologize for what he did. If he is not healthy, he will be insensitive. You need to work towards bringing compassion in your mind and learn that these traits of the other person are often what prevent you from speaking your truth. You get to be more honest with yourself this way.

Be Aware of the Shadows of Shame and How They Undermine Your Ability to See Your Worth

If you don't know where your problems are coming from, you will never know the solution. The solution always goes back to the trauma that was experienced by you as a child. To evoke the repressed experience of any individual, a person locks away the horrific and traumatic memories in order to not deal with them. The mind acts like a circuit breaker that shuts everything down, and it puts the memories in little packets and stores them in the back of their minds.

Codependency is cured by tapping into this psychological energy. Key embodiments to the language of any relationship is the premise of asking, taking, receiving, sharing, refusing, imagining, and giving. It is about asking yourself just how comfortable you in are asking for something, or does it make you feel too dependent? Does it make you subjugate? Do you feel people don't care about what you ask for because you are invisible to them, and it may seem unimportant?

Then you also need to evaluate whether you are a giver. Do you enjoy giving? Do you feel exuberance in your generosity? Can you receive a compliment? Does it feel good or do you start to qualify it? How vulnerable do you feel when you receive one? Is it easy for you to share, or do you find it massively scary and threatening? If you sit down to ask yourself about each of these verbs and check your stance in each situation, you can get a pretty good portrait of yourself.

You need to evaluate which one of the above needs the most focus on and building around. Seek that one person who can hear you out and guide you through this process. Who is the person who wants to give to you, yet you have been shutting them down? Who is that person who you want to give to and share something with? It goes from looking at the map of yourself to identify the core resource and strength that you need to muscle around, and then actually act on it. Attachment in the life of a person can be secure, insecure, or anxious.

You need to be able to rely on someone who can share your distress and your joy, and can respond to it appropriately without neglect, overemphasis on themselves, or without pretending that it's for you when it is actually for them. A secure attachment is when we have a person who provides us with enough bandwidth to explore and are there for us, and your relationship won't fall apart no matter what. If this is missing from a person's life, they may develop insecure attachments. It can be constant checking on the other person, going after them, picking fights to grab attention and so on.

Our attachments today are adaptive of the moment we were experiencing something bad earlier in our lives. It is adaptive and not a problem. It becomes a problem when you start doing this with someone who genuinely cares about you, loves you dearly, and you are still responding to them from the place of your past where you learned it's better to stay distant to keep yourself safe. Usually, the strategies that we devised at the time to deal with a certain situation were useful then, but may become redundant now.

Acknowledging and Embracing All Their Feelings of Betrayal and Hurt

There is a core fear of being perpetually alone. Some of this is about real isolation, abandonment, and rejection. We aren't afraid of being alone on a day to day basis, we are afraid of our feelings. We are afraid of that deep dark place of emptiness, and how it makes us feel so alone.

You can't go to this dark place alone. It may even bring back the fears of your childhood, so you are entering the fears of your five-year-old self and those moments of complete disconnection, when you realize you are alone here. This is a place where you were rejected and abandoned by your loved ones, and that is very painful to deal with.

This activates the core primal survival fear in your mind, where you become desperate to have a connection. If you don't have a connection and sturdy relationship to depend on, you fear you will have a complete meltdown. It is the fear that you will come undone and life will become too frightening. You need to put blinders on. You need to buffer yourself from this potential reality.

The thing to note, we can move beyond fear that is based upon seeing situations through the lens of our history. We try to see it as neutrally as possible from a self-place of a contemplative observer, in order to access reality. It is there we can see that we are not surprised that some people are in relationships, and some are not. Some people feel connected and some don't.

If we are able to be honest with that reality, and we start to believe that it's no big deal if I am going to be alone for the rest of my life, something great happens. You suddenly have a choice. There is spaciousness and freedom. You can begin to not be frightened by that whole idea. You begin to put things in perspective, and it's not that shocking.

The focus now shifts from being alone to accepting that if you are going to be alone, what is it that you want to do for the next thirty years of your life? It's up to you if you want to frame it from the point of view of something that is missing in your life, or whether you are ready to expand your understanding of yourself and learn to invest in family relationships, friendships, and love for the community.

While life doesn't happen to you in the way that you thought it would, you still have a lot of life left to live—where there are endless opportunities and hundreds of ways that you can shape your life—whether you are with or without someone. Nobody is strong enough to take this opportunity away from you.

There is no need to be bogged down from the perspective of not finding a perfect relationship. There is another set of ways to experience life differently. It might not be your first choice, but it's guaranteed that it can still be rich and fulfilling. Don't be so rigid about the way your relationship needs to look. It might not come in the form of a relationship or a partner, and learn to accept that that is not tragic.

Understand How Partners Engage in Codependent Relationships

Your relationship needs repair, and working on your relationship means working on yourself. It is all about having a plan for where you are focusing your healing efforts. Self-directed healing is a lifestyle.

It is about participating consciously in your maturing growth. It is realizing when we are coming from a centered place of clarity and awareness, and how we can educate ourselves better. This will wake us up from old patterns of denial that we have been breeding in ourselves for a long time. You have experienced attachment trauma. It triggers your nervous system, and it creates a hormonal cocktail in your mind, one of distress and fear.

Emotional intimacy also becomes a trigger. The field of vulnerability is very challenging. We often bump into core beliefs of how we are not lovable, or the thought that our partner is going to leave anyway. This relationship is not going to work out. This leads to more anxiety, and a self-fulfilling prophesy where our relationships don't work out.

You can be in your grieving process of, "Here we go again!" or you might be in the middle of your relationship. Yet, you are experiencing an incredible amount of distress, distrust, and confusion. The way to deal with this is to work through it, manage it by not shutting it down, and continue to try to chase happiness with mindfulness.

We are entering a conscious grief process, and that is healing. Self-healing is tapping into your innate wisdom—a place that is coming from feeling grounded—and making choices. It is very much about the agency. Agency is about asserting your will, and realizing that you can impact your immediate and future situation by participating consciously, and then putting forth the effort to create some change. It is a very proactive approach to participate in your life.

It is necessary to address your suffering head-on. It is not going to disappear on its own. Attachment trauma is not going to magically disappear from your nervous system because over time, you have already ignored it enough. We need to vow to participate proactively.

We are going to stop following the codependent approach of waiting for someone else to heal us. We will be proactive. People may confuse this with mentally pulling yourself up by the bootstraps. It means that you need self-endorsement, which is a kind of isolation where you figure it out all alone in your mind, and you keep it to yourself.

It is an internal process, and you still need an external process. We still need education, healing helpers, and a way to find encouragement and nourishment beyond what we are generating for ourselves internally. But we need to come from a grounded place, where we are collaborators and co-creators with all other people who are providing us with this nourishment.

Healing attachment injuries don't happen in a vacuum. We need corrective experiences, where we can engage emotionally and experiment with vulnerability. It's not just limited to family members, loved ones, or partners. We can do this with friends as well.

A good way to do this is by finding a community, a place where you belong. We need to know that we are not alone in what we are going through. At the same time, we need to have a definitive plan of what we are going to do, how we will proceed, understand what is getting in our way, and what outcome we are focusing on, as opposed to being in a permanent state of confusion or being passive, where you are being told what to do. It is about acting, and not just sitting back and reading posts or observing on the sideline.

Self-directed healing keeps track of our goals and monitors whether we are treading in the right direction. Don't give yourself a hard time if you meet an obstacle, challenge, or a limitation. We are constantly adjusting and looking to reach a point where you strengthen yourself, and indulging in self-care and paying attention to the process makes it more workable.

We aren't directly looking at getting fixed. We are looking at just the next step that is going to give you some direction and clarity around your healing process. You have to define what that process is.

To understand this better, we view the concept of therapy without thinking of it as a stale and mundane process. Instead, you need to be active and challenge the whole therapy process. Challenge the therapist and bring in synergy and energy, bring about collaborations, etc.

It is a dynamic process. It is not a stale process of sitting back and having conversations on a couch. It is more about defining what you are doing today, and what is on the horizon for you to achieve immediately.

To stay motivated, you can journal various themes in a day, such as, "What is your prime focus in healing?' Think about a simple task that you can perform today, or this week, which is directed towards your healing. Then you need to write about any obstacle you may face in completing the aforementioned task.

Finally, you can think about your real-time progress through this process. You don't need to write idealized tasks such as 'find peace'. It is not concrete. You need to very specifically name what gives you peace. It may be traveling, reading a book, painting, or anything to this effect.

Developing the Mind-Body-Spirit Connection

Self-love is the idea that love yourself first before you can love another, or you have to love yourself to be eligible to get love from others. This can be confusing and unhelpful for some. Self-love is inherently important for everyone, especially when you have a history of not knowing your sense of self, and not having a strong sense of self.

Self-love is about having a healthy and positive regard for yourself. It is the ability to know that you can hold yourself in esteem, reassuring yourself with a sense of self-worth. If self-love is not fully present, you are unable to assert your likes and dislikes. In relationships, you will find yourself meshing and merging, and not having good emotional boundaries. This is because you are taking on either the concept of who you perceive you are supposed to be, which is a kind of false self, or you find yourself trying to adapt and to take on who the other person is.

There is also a kind of people-pleasing component where you want to show yourself in the best light so it's kind of like where you are asking about people how they would like you to be. You tell them that you can be what they want you to be. I am a chameleon and I will adapt. If you do this enough, there is a quality of betrayal to yourself since you are betraying whom you need to be. The real question that arises here is how you can be more truthful in your presentation of yourself in this world and how you embody and how you feel that you know who you are. You can lead from this place and you are not confused about having a strong sense of self.

The chances are that you grew up in a family where there was a certain amount of dysfunction and a certain amount of non-relating, where you had to accommodate other people's emotional needs and dysfunction in a way to get your emotional needs met. You may have had to deny certain parts of yourself, just to get a place of engaging with a loved one, or engaging with a family member.

Codependency involves over-dependence on others. You're unable to stay grounded and true to your own experience of self. When you betray yourself enough, you disconnect from knowing who you are. The byproduct is that you are not holding yourself in a high enough positive regard, and your conclusion is that you don't love yourself.

There is love, and there is an application of kindness, compassion, gentleness, giving yourself the benefit of doubt, and being able to accommodate, knowing your experiences. This is the love part of self-love. Then there is self, there is knowing that you matter, you are valid, and you are good enough.

We take this whole dynamic and conclude to say... love yourself. In healing communities, when we are trying to address codependency, the pendulum swings in a rather extreme way. If we keep saying the mantra of self-love, it becomes too rigid. It pits emotional connection with others against the relationship of how we feel about ourselves as being primary, and having a connection and love and support from others as being secondary. This setup is very dangerous. It goes against the reality of being a human being. You need both.

You do need a plan to cultivate self-love. This is a healing chapter. It is necessary to create strong boundaries from all these other distractions, and begin to return to who are you. That is at the core of what it means to love yourself.

It's this constant inquiry into who you are, who you have been, how you feel about yourself, and to be able to say, no matter what the experience is, that you are doing fine. You accept everything that is happening to you and around you, all of the rage and craziness, joys and embarrassing moments, etc. You merge it all together, and adapt to it and make yourself feel good and normal about it.

Even though some things may be bothering you, collectively you are still embracing everything that is thrown at you by life. However, you cannot stay in this place forever or think this is the only way to be. We need connections beyond just self-love. There is so much clatter in the self-help community. Everything we read points to the need for us to love ourselves.

It sets a tone where only self-love seems primary, and receiving emotional connection, support, and being in healthy and emotional relationships with other people is not as important. But we equally need to maintain both. We also need to know how to let in nurturing from other relationships.

These emotional concepts shouldn't be pitted against each other, because no one aspect is better than the other. You need positive feedback, encouragement, support, kindness, connection, and resonance from people who care about who we are, and people who love us. The help goes into the garden, and with nourishment, the garden grows. That's how you grow a stronger sense of self.

Join a Group That Focuses on Codependency Recovery

If someone says they are traumatized, we want to focus on the event. That is how they got to know about the existence of problems such as PTSD, codependency, and so on. Our brain returns back to what happened. Perhaps there was an accident, there was sexual abuse, etc. Sometimes there are things that overwhelm us in a way that it is difficult to recover from them. If you are a soldier and you have been in war, and experience various battles, this is termed as a traumatic experience.

It is not necessary for every person who has been in a traumatic experience to suffer from post-traumatic disorder. With more material being available now, and having in-depth knowledge about neuroscience and how the brain functions, it has become very clear that it is not always just the event or a certain happening, that causes symptoms of attachment trauma looping in your nervous system.

So, we move aside the event and actually focus on the person's ability to integrate what is happening around them in their daily lives—the intensity with which they are reacting to a particular situation. If they are unable to integrate the moment and what is going on inside you, your body is not able to come back into equilibrium. The body gets stuck by looping at the same place. They suffer from this chronic stress that is taking over them. The link is in the word *chronic*.

Attachment trauma is the quality of bonding that we have with people that we love. Our survival is dependent on staying connected to the people whom we love. Our survival is dependent on feeling close to the people we love.

Developmental trauma comes from attachment injuries where the injuries are like incidents. We look at what happened, when it happened, and the kind of impact it had in our lives. There is a heightened sense of insecurity around relationships, and this insecurity is not simply just the idea that you are feeling insecure. It is a reference that the quality, strength, and complexity of the bond is compromised. You feel anxious about whether it is safe to be in a relationship with a person.

Can you trust this level of vulnerability? Is this person really available to you? Can we trust this? Will you end up feeling neglected, abandoned, or rejected? This stirs the nervous system. It can skew your perception of reality and can make you susceptible to primal panic.

You have this experience where a relationship equals an insecure attachment. The place of trauma is stored where you experience intimacy. By talking to people constantly about relationship trauma, you get a sense that you are not alone. We need to grieve to really heal.

If you want to leave those old patterns and really begin a life of self-reflection, being conscious, and changing your feelings, it is going to bring up the past and it becomes a grieving process. This can end up in filling us with knowledge about ourselves, feeling inspired, and rejuvenated. This can be called zesty living. We need to confront our core feelings about ourselves.

When people are facing a situation of leaving the narcissist or the narcissist leaves them, they get back into feeling lonely. This loneliness is their number one withdrawal symptom. Codependency is necessarily an addiction because to feel real euphoria, a codependent needs a relationship with a narcissist.

They feel like they have a place on this Earth. They belong to someone, even though that person is troubled. The narcissist uses disappearing acts or silent treatments to punish you. They don't care for you. They just want to cause you pain so that you beg and plead to end emotional pain, and have you give in to their demands. When the codependent does this, the manipulator is not hurting.

Freeze is when you pause, unable to move no matter how much you want to. Most codependents have been on the receiving end of the narcissist's cold, dark, and empty soul.

When you look straight at it the first time, it sends shivers down the spine. Most of us freeze.

You get a feeling that something bad is about to happen and you just can't move. Over time, this passes and some of us learn to get out of it. On looking back, it might feel stupid for letting yourself get in that deep, for not walking away sooner. You can't change what you didn't know. This is not your fault.

If you ultimately decide to make a positive change in knowing everything about yourself and changing the course of your life, you can join recovery communities where you learn that you are not alone in your struggles. The more you seek help and provide your knowledge to others, the better it will make you.

Increase Understanding of Addiction and Codependency

You can indulge in reading and understanding these conditions. These roles play, and ultimately feed into, the victim's consciousness. Victim consciousness means you can't take accountability for what you do. You have such a short-term focus that you can't think of the bigger picture. You can't ever question why you react to the situation in this dramatic way.

When conflict arises, it is so much easier to cry and make everyone feel sorry for you than to consider why on Earth you might be reacting to this situation in such a dramatic way. It's so much easier to use tools of manipulation to get what we want, which is called anxiety alleviation.

You should engage in emotionally honest dialogues. Instead of manipulating your partner who is going out, tell them you are feeling really insecure, and ask their opinion on this. You don't want to manipulate them. You really want them to come back to you. So, practicing this can help you understand the perspective of the other side, and really help to understand how the other person may be viewing you as a persecutor, instead of as a poor, innocent victim.

This is more personal accountability, because the co-creators are constantly assuring that the creator is being their best self and is not pandering to their victim. After you assume responsibility on how you are communicating with your peers, you can move to trauma alleviation. They want an equal distribution of respect, love, and care in their relationships, but they don't know how to get it. The want of equality ties them to the relationship.

They are with a person who is unable to reciprocate their feelings. They resent that person, and yet maintain the relationship. There can be an active codependent who pursues another person who tries to control them, but both share the same psychological and relational traits. They stay in a relationship, and freely and abundantly gives to others, while not getting the same.

The term codependency has been overused and can be harmful in the way people use it. It has been morphed into a stereotype. Codependents are individuals who have problems, they feel stuck, hurt, and ignored.

It is very important to recognize that they have a disorder. They are struggling to find care, love, and respect, but can't find it. We first have to learn how to do it for our own selves. It is necessary to have this sense of self-validation, so that when we receive this compliment from someone it feels good, but not amazing. What should feel amazing is the validation you give to your own self. I got up early, went to the office, came back, cleaned, cooked dinner, and ate. I am amazing! I can do it and more. That's an amazing person right there.

When you start applying this in your life, you will soon come to realize how seldom you are seeking that validation from others now. Even if there is physical abuse, how narcissists blame shifts, or uses reactive abuse against codependents is very difficult to comprehend. It is equally hard to discuss it with people. Sexual abuse is also very difficult to open up about

You are not now, nor were you ever crazy. You just loved, cared, trusted, and respected the toxic words of a manipulator. You can never have enough knowledge to understand who they are, or what they do... and there are always some red flags. The toxicity chips away at our confidence and self-worth, leaving us questioning our own instincts. They make us believe we are not lovable and should be grateful for the narcissist's negative and toxic love.

Once you do start to see, you can start putting reality back into your own mind, creating your own thoughts, and thinking for yourself again. Learning and understanding this disorder can guide you to know how to feel far from crazy. You are just being manipulated by someone to feel that way, so that they could keep control over you.

Learning those insecurities are actually your instincts speaking out. Even though at the time you didn't know what they were telling you, now you know your instincts are telling you something. Trust it—as it's usually right.

From one moment to the next, you are just oblivious as to whether they are going to have us walking on eggshells around them, tiptoeing around the landmine, in case we set them off. In reality, it is not all that sets them off. It's who they are. They set themselves off. This doesn't make it easy.

After time, you start to understand that it's all to manipulate you into getting their own needs met. They don't care for other people's needs. It's all to distort your reality and your perceptions of them. It is all to train your mind to behave how they want you to.

They need to be able to control others, as they don't truly know what they want out of their lives. They feed off others. No matter what you do, it will never be right. They cause fear in your mind to question your abilities, to fear to be open ourselves around others, to be scared of what people will think about you, to worry about offending other people, to worry about other people's reactions to you just being yourself. Learn to re-create yourself to be exactly who you are or who you want to be. Rediscover yourself, removing self-doubt from your mind with positive intention.

Decide if it is worth forgiving. This step is the most important: before recovering, you need to understand whether it is important. No matter how much you love them: to forgive a betrayal is the most difficult challenge you can ever face.

Here are some possible reasons to forgive: It happened only once. Maybe you had a fight, and after drinking one glass too many, they ended up in bed with another person. Your partner is really sorry for what happened, is depressed, and would do anything to prove their repentance. If you think you have a really special relationship, you may want to resist the temptation to leave, to see if you can recover it.

You don't want to give up your relationship, especially if you've been with this person for a long time and your relationship is healthy and intimate. Discovering a betrayal, of course, will put all this in doubt. You should analyze the whole story before making a decision. Don't forgive a serial traitor. If they have already done it, and you have children and a life together, it's not worth it.

Maybe it's only the first time you have caught them, but they have betrayed you many times already. Do not forgive a betrayal if you are with this new person: it will be almost impossible to build a solid relationship on this foundation. If betrayal is a sign of a relationship destined to fail, do not try hard. Two people who have nothing in common, who do not feel very attracted to each other, and who are unable to make the relationship work, have no future.

Think about your relationship after you've calmed down. How are you with this person? Imagine a future together. Is it an important relationship, or are you just afraid of losing it?

Here are some more questions: What's special about this relationship? Are you willing to forgive this person because you want to be seriously together, or because you don't want to be alone? If you realize that your relationship is based on nothing, put an end to it.

How would you describe the trajectory of the relationship? Were things going well for a while and then got worse, or was it always an alternation of ups and downs? Try to find the reasons why the relationship is no longer what it was before. Why did your partner betray you? Think of the negative contributions of both. They were jealous of you, or you were together from high school and they started to believe that they settled too soon.

You will both have to acknowledge your feelings and accept the pain and confusion. Tell them how you feel, and make sure they understand what is happening to you. Before you can recover the relationship, your partner will have to understand that they have put you in a terrible position.

Work on having more open communication every day: Talk about the status of the report at least once a week. This step should not be forced, but do not underestimate it. Tell yourself how you feel. Talk about both positive and negative emotions, even if you have distanced yourself after the betrayal. Don't be passive-aggressive. If you are angry, say it when it's time.

Seek Counseling from a Licensed and Qualified Therapist Who is Familiar with Codependency

Codependency can be extremely emotional, and as such, may cause depression, anxiety, anger, or resentment. It can be social on account of loss of a friend. It can be physical or occupational. Codependents are reflexively and magnetically attracted to narcissists. One is a caregiver and the other is a caretaker, and they both fit perfectly in this dysfunctional relationship that requires their opposite personality to keep them together.

But when you break free from this dance, and you challenge the person by disagreeing with them, the narcissist tends to not have the ability to accept fault in the problems. They tend to get very angry, feel betrayed, and they blame the person who is blaming them. They fail to see what's wrong with themselves, but can always see what's wrong with others.

The codependent needs to acclimate to the narcissist's injuries, guilt trip, shaming, and allegations of being selfish. Once they become accustomed to it and start to predict, it they start to feel more confident, with fewer negative thoughts and fears. Over time, they become more and more confident. They set their boundaries without the fear of someone not wanting to be in a relationship with them.

Codependency before their recovery would not allow them to set boundaries because of the fear of being alone. In stage two, the boundaries are set because they know that having a healthy relationship is far more important than the anxiety, fear, and grief. It is necessary to find a qualified therapist in your area who can be your accomplice in the disorder, and help you come out of it. A lot depends on the therapy you are undergoing.

Practice Mindfulness and Self-Compassion

To really understand how mindfulness and self-compassion are related, we start by understanding compassion. Compassion is concerned with the lifting of suffering, including sufferings that one experiences deep within them. There are three sets of different components for others and yourself. The initial aspect of compassion is awareness and mindfulness. To really open our hearts in the face of suffering, we need to be insightfully aware that suffering has been occurring, and we need to turn it around. Otherwise we won't be able to embrace it in the arms of compassion.

Another important component is being kind to yourself and others. This is fairly obvious, and a salient component of compassion. It's about treating others and yourself with care and understanding, which is also the active part of compassion, where you are concerned with the alleviation of suffering. There is a motivation to do something about suffering.

Kindness therefore entails active, soothing support and comfort. When your friend comes to you and tells you a story of suffering, you might try to make them know through your actions that you care. The next step is to show humanity.

We usually separate ourselves from others, and this detachment of self helps us experience the others person's life. However, we need to have a sense of mutuality. The sense of everyone belonging and not judging anyone for their actions.

The difference between mindfulness and compassion really depends on how you use the term mindfulness. The most common definition used in this field is paying attention to our present moment's experience with a sense of acceptance, non-judgment, and friendship. There is one more place in which the term eternal awareness of mind is used. It is applicable, but is different than the previous definition.

Mindfulness is used as an inclusive term for the contemplative practice or path of waking to the needs of our hearts and minds. There are aspects that come under mindfulness. The first aspect is how we converge all our efforts into this present moment, which is observing what's going on as it is happening.

The next component is how we engage with the present moment. We take it on without any problem or hatred, and with acceptance. The third aspect is compassion. Compassion is focused at the experiencer.

Mindfulness has to do with being aware of what is happening around you without judging. Compassion requires the art of being, and it is focused on the concern of suffering. Another mandatory aspect is wisdom. It is about focusing on the nature of both the person who is experienced and the person who is the experiencer.

It is about understanding that the event is impermanent. It begins, and then slowly vanishes away. As experiencers, we are not really as different and alone as we may perceive ourselves to be. We are essentially a part of a larger, interdependent whole.

All these intuitive factors of mindfulness are cumulative and kind of depend on one other. Time truly heals. It's about attaining maturity and controlling your emotions from getting the best of you in the situation.

Once your partner cheats, the adrenaline rush that flows through the body makes them either shut down or become violently aggressive. You can get drawn into these emotions, and they may get you as far down as wishing to end your life. But what is important at those moments, is to just hold on to something positive within you. It shouldn't be external, but rather, it has to be internal. A strong mind, and a drive to live a better life independently, must motivate you to reach a better phase in your life. Take this as an experience where you learn something, and not let it paralyze or scar you for good.

This is not the only relationship that you will have in your life. You need to work towards getting your confidence back and know your worth. No one should be so important that they claim a right over your life. Everyone is sufficient for themselves.

The feeling of ending up alone is an irrational fear that the mind creates, and the other person becomes irreplaceable. However, they can be replaced by someone capable of loving you even more than them, and you can have the life you deserve with them.

You need to look at the big picture so that you are able to experience emotional awakening and really open up your mind. A codependent is supposed to embrace these aspects in order to reach new levels of intimacy with others, and have a spiritual awakening to everything that they experienced in the past, and learn to integrate it, normalize it, and move on.

True forgiveness is removing all the pain, and traces of the pain, from both the outer world, and the inner world as well. To forgive you completely they need to get rid of all the remains of the pain surrounding what caused the hurt. It has to be unconditional.

This is the ultimate goal. It is achievable.

There has to be genuine remorse and a genuine want to not hurt the person anymore. If you do have a pattern of repeating what causes your partner to get hurt, you need to identify the cause that's stirring you to do it. You need to repair that element. It's not about dealing with forgiveness, it's about dealing with the pattern.

Certain myths need to be busted when dealing with the gray area. To think that time will heal, and the relationship will become restored to its formal glory is true to some extent. This can often be used as an excuse by a person to not do much. The person just wallows in self-pity.

Like any change, healing from hurt cannot be done instantly. To do that there has to be the right environment and the right mindset, and you can heal fairly quickly. You need to give it as much time as it needs. The process can be sped up, depending on what you do and how you do it.

Chapter 6: Conclusion

Codependents always feel like it's their responsibility to keep everything right in their relationship. They feel that their value in the relationship comes from being able to fix or save the other person, to get them through their problems, or even clean up their mess. They may do anything to hold on to the relationship even though it's unsafe or destructive. They are willing to compromise a lot that they would not normally, because it feels like it's what they need to do to hang on to the relationship, because they don't actually believe that they can survive alone.

They may be willing to not speak up, not set a boundary, or not assert their own wants or preferences on the other person because when they do, they feel guilty. They refrain from making the relationship about them in any way. People can find themselves in unhealthy and unbalanced relationships. They receive nothing in return.

Despite the pain, they stay in this unhappy and toxic relationship. This comes from intense shame and pathological loneliness. Even though we call it codependency, it is actually depravity of love for self. Codependency is a symptom of not loving one's self. It doesn't need to be treated. But the root cause needs to be addressed.

The attachment trauma as we discussed hinders them from feeling loved and cared for. This trauma causes them core shame. It is a distorted belief that they are fundamentally bad or flawed. Such toxic shame reduces the person to feel good only when they take care of others and ignore themselves. Loving someone while being invisible creates a loneliness that puts the person through excruciating pain and reduces them to feeling invisible, worthless, and unlovable. The pain is simply unbearable.

That is why they become addicted to the relationship that will make the lonely pain go away. The narcissistic love becomes their drug of choice. It will never remedy their loneliness and lifelong pursuit of love and care. This turns them into a compulsive caretaker who habitually attempts to control others into loving them. The problem is never codependency, it is what lies beneath it.

This invisible and treatment-resistant addiction can't be remedied unless its underlying causes are addressed. The way to get over this situation is by creating self-love abundance. First, the root of the problem is addressed. The person, in their therapy, safely explores all the repressed issues. By bringing their hurt child experiences forward, they are able to accept the sad reality of their childhood, let it go, and integrate it into their conscious mind.

This allows them to realize core self-love. It is a realistic and optimistic, self-affirming definition of love which is based on what is naturally and fundamentally good about a person. This leads to existential peace.

For the first time, the newly self-loving person feels comfortable in their own skin, free from shame and loneliness. This person can then find and demand mutuality and reciprocity in all their relationships. There are newly defined rules in their relationships which are self-respect, self-worth, and self-love. The person finally achieves serenity and acceptance of one's place in the world. Being perfect despite one's problems is the foundation for future loving relationships with self and with others.

I wish you luck and hope this reading has helped you understand and manage codependency.

Thank you for purchasing this book and I hope that reading it has been an interesting and educational experience. I put all my efforts, enthusiasm and heart into every sentence I write. The main goal of this book is to help my readers with my experience.

If you liked it, and above all, it influenced your life and helped you along the way, I ask you for five minutes of your time to write what you think of the book by leaving a review, because it would help other people improve their lives. The opinions of my readers are always valuable for my work and would help me improve the way I communicate and would give me new ideas to develop.

www.ingramcontent.com/pod-product-compliance
Lightning Source LLC
Chambersburg PA
CBHW071804080526
44589CB00012B/674